British Railways
The First 25 Years

Volume 2
The West Midlands

Stanier Class '5' No. 44818 pounds up the Lickey incline with a northbound train, assisted by '9F' banker No. 92079. The seven ex-L&NER coaches and three BR Mark 1s, all in 'blood & custard' livery, indicate a date of 1956 or 1957. No. 44818 was from Derby shed, moving to Saltley in November 1959.

BRITISH RAILWAYS

The First 25 Years

Volume 2 – The West Midlands

J. Allan and A. Murray

Lightmoor Press

BR Sulzer Type '2' No. D5010, which had probably arrived on a stopping train from Rugby, alongside 'Britannia' No. 70016 *Ariel* on a Manchester express at Birmingham New Street in August 1964. The diesel was then allocated to Rugby, having spent three years on loan to the Southern Region, while the 'Brit', originally a Western Region engine, had been at Aston shed since June 1963. In the background is the Rotunda tower, which was opened in early 1965.

'King' Class 4-6-0 No. 6002 *King William IV* with the 11.10am Paddington-Birkenhead arriving at Leamington on 9th July 1961.

© Lightmoor Press, J. Allan & A. Murray, 2013
Reprinted 2019
Designed by Stephen Phillips

British Library Cataloguing-in-Publication Data.
A catalogue record for this book is available from the British Library.
ISBN 9781899889 78 5

LIGHTMOOR PRESS
Unit 144B, Lydney Trading Estate, Harbour Road, Lydney, Gloucestershire GL15 5EJ
www.lightmoor.co.uk
Lightmoor Press is an imprint of Black Dwarf Lightmoor Publications Ltd.

Printed in Poland
www.lfbookservices.co.uk

Contents

The pictures in this book cover the area of England centred on Birmingham, extending to Rugby and Leamington in the south, and to Wolverhampton and Stafford in the north.

Crewe North 'Royal Scot' No. 46136 *The Border Regiment* on a north-bound express at Stafford in 1961. Note the Southern Railway designed 4-wheeled utility van at the head of the train; non-passenger carrying vehicles were a regular feature of expresses on this route, often used to convey Irish boat traffic luggage.

Introduction and acknowledgements

This is the second in a series of books, depicting the first twenty-five years of British Railways, which will eventually cover the whole of Great Britain. We have been fortunate to have had access to hundreds of different pictures from which to choose the final selection presented here. At an early stage we made the decision to include photographs spanning the early British Railways era through to the pre-TOPS diesels, although the emphasis is on that interesting transitional period of the late 1950s and early 1960s.

This volume covers the West Midlands, essentially the county of Warwickshire and then over the border in the north and west to Staffordshire, and in the south west just in to Worcestershire. We start on the London Midland Region at Rugby, following the two main ex-L&NWR routes as far as Stafford on the West Coast main line, and to Coventry and Birmingham New Street. Next is the former Midland Railway Burton to Birmingham line and then a long stay at New Street itself, before examining two of the London Midland's suburban routes. Then we move on to the Western Region line from Leamington to Birmingham, stopping off for a good look at Snow Hill station and its suburban route into Warwickshire. Heading north again from Birmingham we follow the alternative routes into the Black Country from Snow Hill and New Street, and then explore the Western Region lines from Wolverhampton into the Black Country. Our journey this time is completed by picking up the Midland Railway line again at New Street and heading south west as far south as Bromsgrove and the Lickey Incline.

We have attempted to produce a mix which we hope everyone will like, with main line, station and depot shots, including a number of industrial locations. We have also put together several features using groups of pictures; these include the rebuilding of Birmingham New Street station, the movement of 'Coronation' 'Pacific' *City of Birmingham* through the streets of the city and the operation of the Lickey incline. Since one of the authors lives in the Sutton Coldfield area, we have indulged in a detailed study of two local suburban lines, one of which from Birmingham to Lichfield has prospered as part of the electrified 'Cross City' route, while the other is now a freight only line around the eastern side of the city from Castle Bromwich and Water Orton to Bescot. We have also included a number of pictures taken in the late 1950s and early 1960s on the former Great Western Birmingham to Wolverhampton route at Wednesbury, a location whose industrial landscape was not often photographed.

Our biggest decision having selected the pictures was how to arrange them and here we have combined geography with 'time travel' to produce what we think is an interesting and reasonably logical ordering of the material. So join us as we start our journey. We will of course stop off to 'bunk' some of the main sheds en route and also call in at Wolverhampton Stafford Road Works.

The majority of the pictures in this volume are from the www.Rail-Online.co.uk collection, supplemented to a considerable degree by the work of Robert Darlaston who took many excellent pictures in the area during the 1950s and 1960s. We have also used material from Brian Penney and Michael Mensing who was a prolific photographer of his local West Midlands scene. From time to time we have included full page portraits which pay full tribute to the quality of the photographs taken all those years ago.

Our special thanks go to Mike Hollick for his help with many of the captions, aided and abetted by our old friend Vic Smith. Other valuable contributions have been made by Bob Essery, David Clarke and Colin Moss. Any errors remaining are of course entirely the responsibility of the authors and publishers.

References

We have consulted a number of books to provide details of locomotives and workings and in particular, the RCTS Great Western, BR Standard and LM&SR locomotive histories, the Irwell Press 'Book of' series, the Yeadon L&NER series and *The Allocation History of BR Diesels & Electrics*. We have also used the excellent website 'www.warwickshirerailways.com' for general information on the area and 'www.sixbellsjunction.co.uk' for details of railtours and special workings.

J. Allan
A. Murray
2013

'Coronation' No. 46221 *Queen Elizabeth* with the Down 'Red Rose' from London to Liverpool at Netherstowe Lane near Lichfield in 1962. No. 46221 was the only one of its class which ran with all three types of 10-ton tender, with welded, riveted and part-welded tanks. It was paired with the part-welded tender from No. 46253 *City of St. Albans* between November 1961 and October 1962, and then had the coal-pusher equipped riveted tender from 'Princess Royal' No. 46206 *Princess Helena Victoria* until it was withdrawn in May 1963.

1 – West Coast main line - Rugby to Stafford

The London Midland Region line from Rugby, 82 miles north of London, to Stafford was one of the busiest stretches of double track main line in the country. It had to handle not only the express services from London to Manchester, Liverpool, North Wales and Scotland but also local trains serving the Trent Valley and freight traffic between all these locations. It was opened by the London & North Western Railway in November 1847 as a more direct line to the north instead of the original route through Birmingham and Wolverhampton. There were important junctions at Nuneaton, Tamworth and Lichfield, where there were four tracks or more, but it was not until 2008 that the whole of the line was quadrupled, with the exception of the short stretch from Colwich where the line to Stoke-on-Trent diverged, through Shugborough Tunnel into Stafford.

Apart from limited signalling and station improvements, little had changed during the first half of the 20th century but when the line between Euston and Crewe was electrified under the British Railways Modernisation Plan of 1955, the infrastructure of the whole of the Trent Valley line was modernised. Multiple aspect colour lights replaced semaphore signalling throughout and the stations at Tamworth and Stafford were completely rebuilt. The work, which began in 1960, took about five years to complete and had to be carried out while services continued, although

there was severe disruption and passenger trains had extensive recovery times added to their schedules. The overhead line wires were energised in stages from the north, starting at Stafford in November 1962 and ending with Rugby in September 1964 but the full electric service through to Euston did not start until April 1966.

The motive power on the line was essentially a continuation of London Midland & Scottish Railway practice until the end of the 1950s, although British Railways did concentrate its handful of diesel prototypes on the route, with the Southern Railway designed No's 10201-3 joining the LM&SR diesels No's 10000-1 and the revolutionary *Deltic* was a regular from 1955 until 1958. The first of the diesels ordered under the Modernisation Plan began to appear in 1959, the cumbersome 'Peaks' and English Electric Type '4's taking over the express workings from the 'Royal Scots' and Stanier 'Pacific's which were reduced to a second string role as steam was displaced. The transition was not finally completed until the second batch of electric locomotives, the 'AL6's, appeared during 1965.

The last 'Royal Scot' to be rebuilt with a taper boiler, No. 46137 *The Prince of Wales's Volunteers (South Lancashire)* passing the Hillmorton masts near Rugby in 1950. It was originally named *Vesta* and was renamed in May 1936. No. 46137 received its British Railways number in May 1948, with a scroll type smokebox numberplate and LM&SR pattern large sized cab numbers. The first vehicle is a LM&SR Period One all-Third coach fitted with Stones ventilators; it has been added as a 'strengthener' to provide additional seating.

Rebuilt 'Royal Scot' No. 46114 *Coldstream Guardsman* photographed from the same spot at Hillmorton as No. 46137. It had been converted in 1946 but was not fitted with smoke deflectors until September 1950. It became No. 46114 in June 1948, with thin block pattern numerals on the numberplate but standard 8ins cab numbers. Allocated to Manchester Longsight until May 1955, it was then transferred to Camden. Just as with No. 46137, an elderly Period One all-Third 'strengthener' has been added at the front of the train.

The two LM&SR-designed diesel-electric prototypes make an interesting contrast with the previous two pictures taken at the same position outside Rugby. The 'terrible twins' are in what looks like an early appearance after heavy general repairs over the winter of 1950-1. No. 10000 has lost the cast 'LMS' letters which it had from new until it went into Derby Works in November 1950.

'Royal Scot' No. 46146 *The Rifle Brigade* in June 1954 at Hillmorton. It carried the name of the old L&NWR engine Jenny Lind up to May 1936. No. 46146 was rebuilt with a taper boiler in October 1943 and was shedded at Camden from March 1954 until 1961.

'Royal Scot' No. 46125 *3rd Carabinier* in July 1959, at Newbold near Rugby on a Down special. It had been a Crewe North engine since March 1954.

'Coronation' No. 46240 *City of Coventry* approaching Rugby from the south in 1961, in its final livery of crimson lake, lined in LM&SR style yellow and black, which it received in August 1960. The fireman is taking a breather as the train slows down for the station. The knotted handkerchief was almost standard headgear for firemen working these Stanier 'Pacific's. No. 46240 was fitted with a Smith-Stone speed indicator in August 1957 and AWS in May 1959.

Rugby

Until the 1960s, Rugby was the junction for seven different lines, of which the West Coast main line through the Trent Valley was the most important. The first station was opened by the London & Birmingham Railway in 1840 but the one which lasted right through the 20th century was opened in 1885. At the south end lines came in from London, Northampton and Market Harborough, and in the north from Birmingham, Leamington, Leicester and Stafford. The track layout was complex and arranged around a single 1,410 feet long island platform, with bay platforms at either end and scissors crossovers to allow two trains to use each platform simultaneously. Up and Down through lines were provided for trains not stopping at the station. The L&NWR built a single twelve-road shed in 1876, which closed in 1965. A second adjoining twelve-road shed was opened in 1886 but this was closed and demolished in 1960. A new diesel shed was built by 1965, utilising one wall of the old Rugby Works, and local diesels were maintained there but the site of the running shed also continued in use for some years stabling diesel shunters.

A nice cameo on 4th April 1961 at Rugby with the driver of the 'Patriot' having a chat with the railwayman on the platform, as the double header, with Class '5' No. 44831 leading, waits to depart. Note the brazier which was supposed to keep the water column from freezing. Unnamed 'Patriot' No. 45549 was one of the final ten engines of the class built at Crewe in 1934, two years after Stanier joined the LM&SR. It was allocated to Warrington Dallam shed from June 1959 until withdrawn in June 1962. The engine's right hand running plate is very cluttered with the AWS battery box, the large sandbox, the AWS cylinder and the mechanical lubricator.

Class '5' No. 44910 at Rugby with, despite the train reporting number, a Down train, taken during 1964 when it was shedded at Bescot. The distinctive canopy supports and water columns were similar at both the north and south ends of the station but at the northern end they were 'ribbed'; other features, such as the positioning of water columns, were very similar.

English Electric Type '4' No. D325, which was built in December 1960, is seen at Rugby in 1961, with the '1A35' 12.25pm Blackpool Central to Euston according to the paper headcode – the headcode box was broken and the staff had reverted back to using paper stickers. The yard to the north of the station often held traffic associated with the cement works at Southam, as demonstrated here with the chalk tippler and hopper wagons.

A pair of BR Sulzer Type '2's, No's D5076 and D5074, on 9th July 1961, parked on the lines leading to the L&NWR shed with the 1886 shed and Works in the background. Both diesels had been delivered to March on the Eastern Region in 1960 but quickly moved to the London Midland, at Watford and Willesden respectively.

Gas turbine No. 18000 on 9th July 1961, in the Rugby Test Plant. It had been ordered by the Great Western Railway from Brown-Boveri in Switzerland and entered service in February 1950. The experiment with this form of traction proved unsuccessful, although No. 18000 was less of a failure than the other gas turbine, No. 18100, built by Metropolitan Vickers around the same time. Condemned at Swindon on 16th December 1960, No. 18000 arrived at Rugby in June 1961, according to *The Railway Observer* 'having apparently been acquired by AEI for test purposes in connection with electrification'. This may have been speculation because No. 18100 had been converted in 1958 for use as a driver training locomotive for the Crewe-Manchester electrification. The locomotive was returned to Swindon until it was sold in 1965 to the International Union of Railways, where it was used in Switzerland for research purposes. Stripped of its turbines and most of its ancillary equipment, it was returned to Britain in 1993 for preservation.

English Electric Type '4' No. D291 threads its way over the north end pointwork with the fourteen coaches of 'The Manxman' from Liverpool to London on 8th August 1961. It had the distinction of being the last Class '40' to be broken up, in December 1988, at Crewe Works by outside contractors.

BR Sulzer Type '2' No. D5011 at Rugby heading for Northampton on 30th January 1963. There are stencilled details showing the tank capacity as these were not initially fitted with gauges; also note the grab rungs on the footholds leading to the steam heat boiler filler. No. D5011 was allocated to Rugby from June 1962, soon after returning from three years on loan to the Southern Region; the first fifteen of the class were sent there to cover late deliveries of new BRC&W Type '3's. It was one of four returned locomotives allocated to Rugby, along with No's D5003/05/17, which were used to replace steam on the local services from there.

Burton 'Jubilee' No. 45579 *Punjab* at Rugby on a snowy Sunday morning on 3rd February 1963, with the 9.0am Rugby-Swanbourne freight. Swanbourne was just outside Bletchley on the Oxford line and, during World War Two, a substantial yard known as Swanbourne Sidings was built 2½ miles north east of the station. The yard remained busy until the 1960s and, indeed, in the 1955 Modernisation Plan it was proposed to expand these sidings into a large marshalling yard but this plan was later abandoned.

An Eastern Region intruder on the West Coast main line, 'O1' 2-8-0 No. 63725 passes the Associated Electrical Industries (AEI) factory at Rugby in 1963, probably working over to Peterborough via Market Harborough. The locomotive had an interesting history, having been built by Robert Stephenson & Hawthorn Ltd for the War Department as ROD No. 1641 in August 1919. It went to the L&NWR a month later as No. 2832, before it was purchased by the L&NER in August 1924, becoming No. 6328. It was rebuilt as an 'O1' in March 1945 at Gorton Works, was renumbered in June 1946 as No. 3725 and finally became British Railways No. 63725 in August 1949. The 2-8-0 was allocated to March in February 1957 and was transferred to Staveley (GC) in November 1963, soon after this picture was taken.

No. 45735 *Comet* leaving Rugby on 30th July 1963, with a fitted freight consisting of container wagons; this is almost certainly one of the daily Holyhead-London Broad Street meat trains. One of the two 'Jubilees' rebuilt with a 'Royal Scot' tapered boiler in 1942, it retains the Stanier cab which made it almost indistinguishable from the rebuilt 'Patriots' which received these cabs when they were fitted with taper boilers. Note that the overhead masts are in place but the wires are not yet up – the work was not completed until November 1963. No. 45735 was coming near to the end of its stay at Willesden, going to Annesley in October, where it spent its final year in service.

Tender first '8F' 2-8-0 No. 48120 at the north end of Rugby, on the remaining spur of the closed Leicester line on 3rd August 1963, shunting cement traffic connected to the works at Southam.

Rebuilt 'Patriot' No. 45527 *Southport* at Rugby Midland north end passing the AEI factory on 3rd August 1963. The rebuilt 'Patriot' was allocated to Willesden for three months in the summer of that year, before moving to Carlisle, where it would see out its days until withdrawn at the end of 1964.

English Electric Type '4' No. D219 on 30th July 1963 leaving Rugby with an Up express underneath the new overhead gantries but before the wires were installed. It had been named *Caronia* a year earlier.

No. E3053 was built by Metropolitan Vickers in January 1962 and designated 'AL2'. It became No. 82007 as Class '82' under TOPS but lasted only until July 1983, having been stored, withdrawn and reinstated in the previous eighteen months. The class of ten 'AL2's was unique among the original five LM electric types, because it had a separate underframe instead of integral construction and also Commonwealth cast steel bogies rather than the fabricated box-section types. The electrification wiring had been completed down to Rugby by November 1963, trial working beginning in early September 1964, with full working commencing at the end of the month.

At Rugby in August 1964, paired with Class '5' No. 45434, Stanier Pacific No. 46256 *Sir William Stanier F.R.S.* works a 49-wagon fitted freight from the London area to Crewe. It would be cleaned and polished before its final run the following month, on the RCTS 'The Scottish Lowlander' railtour, which it worked from Crewe to Carlisle and back.

No. 46240 *City of Coventry* at Rugby Midland on 7th September 1964, seeing out its last month in service on freight duties. It was one of eighteen 'Coronations' withdrawn in the first two weeks of September, leaving only No. 46256 which was retained for the RCTS special on 26th September.

Brinklow

Brinklow was a favourite place for photographing the West Coast main line, with the railway running alongside the Oxford Canal for a short distance. Until the line was rebuilt by Network Rail in 2005-8, there were only three tracks, with an Up goods line which ran from Brinklow station to Attleborough, one mile south of Nuneaton, but no corresponding northbound Slow line.

The LM&SR 'Turbomotive' No. 6202 in early 1948, on a northbound train at Brinklow. It is in LM&SR 1946 lined black livery, which was applied during a Heavy General repair completed in April 1947. No. 6202 was out of traffic with transmission failure from April 1948 until March 1949, after which it was returned to service as 46202.

Now with its BR number, 'Turbomotive' No. 46202 is reflected in the water of the Oxford Canal at Brinklow, wearing the BR lined black received in March 1949. It ran in this livery only until May 1950, suffering several unscheduled repairs in the meantime, and was then taken into Crewe Works where it was rebuilt as a conventional reciprocating engine. Emerging in that form on 13th August 1952, it worked for only eight more weeks before it was damaged beyond repair in the Harrow & Wealdstone accident on 8th October.

The penultimate 'Coronation' No. 46256 *Sir William A. Stanier F.R.S.* heads northbound at Brinklow in 1950 on 'The Midday Scot', which was on this occasion loaded to seventeen coaches. The locomotive entered traffic as an LM&SR engine in December 1947, just two weeks before nationalisation. Its original 1946-pattern lined black livery was replaced by the BR version in October 1948, at the same time as electric lighting was fitted. During 1950, a Smith-Stone speed indicator driven off the rear coupled axle was fitted and a welded pony truck replaced the original fabricated one. No. 46256 was repainted into BR standard blue during a works visit completed in May 1951.

'Jubilee' No. 45574 *India* in 1950, on a southbound express at Brinklow looking smart in BR lined black livery, with the transitional BRITISH RAILWAYS insignia on the Fowler tender, with which it was paired from July 1949. The coaches are mostly in LM&SR livery, although two near the rear of the train have already acquired the new 'blood & custard' livery. India was allocated to Blackpool shed from July 1937 until September 1964.

LM&SR built 'Compound' 4-4-0 No. 41090 at Brinklow in 1950. It was allocated to Rugby at this date, moving to Monument Lane in July 1951 and lasted until December 1958. No. 41090 is on a Down local formed of a three coach LM&SR suburban non-corridor set with, strangely, a Stanier corridor all-Third at the rear.

Crewe South Stanier 2-6-0 No. 42980 heads south at Brinklow in 1950, with what the headlamps denote as a Class 'H' unfitted freight that is rather unusually made up entirely of sheeted merchandise opens. The 'Mogul' had been at 5B since 1941 and gained its BR number in October 1949.

Above: Stanier 2-cylinder 2-6-4T No. 42627 on a northbound local at Brinklow in 1950. The locomotive had been renumbered in March 1950 during a Heavy Intermediate repair at Crewe. No. 42627 was allocated to Ryecroft shed at Walsall from June 1945 until June 1958, when it was transferred to Bangor. Note the barge making its way along the canal in the right background.

Unnamed 'Patriot' 4-6-0 No. 45513 in 1950 at Brinklow, on a northbound milk train including a 6-wheeled tank and an L&NWR 6-wheeled van. This engine was allocated to Crewe from January 1950.

Above: Shedded at Crewe North from June 1950 until November 1952, 'Patriot' 4-6-0 No. 45502 *Royal Naval Division* is seen at Brinklow with a southbound express in the early 1950s. It received its BR number in November 1948. The 'stock board' used to fit train reporting numbers on the smokebox door is attached to the handrail only at its top edge and has been flipped up.

Below: 'Royal Scot' No. 46110 *Grenadier Guardsman* with a Down express at Brinklow in 1950. It received its BR number in April 1949 and was rebuilt in January 1953.

Above: Rebuilt 'Royal Scot' No. 46101 *Royal Scots Grey* on an Up express, with an unusual suffix to the train reporting number – 'London' in vertical lettering. This engine was one of a handful of 'Scots' which were given self-cleaning smokeboxes, hence the 'SC' plate below the shedplate. These were not successful because they had an adverse effect on the steaming and it appears that only a handful of the rebuilt engines were modified. No. 46101 was converted to taper boiler in November 1945 and was fitted with smoke deflectors in August 1949.

Below: Rebuilt with a tapered boiler in August 1947, 'Patriot' 4-6-0 No. 45528, seen in 1950 on an Up express at Brinklow, is in very unkempt LM&SR black and still with 'LMS' on the tender, although it had been renumbered in March 1949. It did not receive its smoke deflectors until July 1952. No. 45528 was allocated to Crewe North from March 1950 until February 1955, albeit punctuated by three short vacations at Camden in the intervening years. It was named *R.E.M.E.* (the abbreviation for the Royal Electrical & Mechanical Engineers) in October 1959, apparently as the result of a staff suggestion at Crewe.

Above: Parallel boiler 'Royal Scot' No. 46164 *The Artists Rifleman* from Liverpool Edge Hill, with an Up express at Brinklow in 1950. It is in LM&SR 1946 lined black with BRITISH RAILWAYS on the tender and was rebuilt with a taper boiler the following June.

No. 46200 *The Princess Royal* leaves a comprehensive smoke trail behind at Brinklow in 1950. It had been renumbered in August 1948 at the end of a Heavy Scheduled overhaul, during which a domed boiler was fitted. Apart from the new cabside numerals and smokebox door numberplate, the engine and tender are still in 1946 lined black LM&SR livery that was already well worn but which would have to last until 1952.

No. 46204 *Princess Louise* in 1950, on a Down express alongside the Oxford Canal at Brinklow. It had been renumbered in April 1948 with 10ins LM&SR 1946 style numerals and a scroll & serif smokebox plate but these had both been changed to the BR standard pattern by the time this photograph was taken. Incredibly, No. 46204 kept its pre-war LM&SR crimson lake paintwork which apparently was not replaced until 1952, although it was fitted with a domed boiler in September 1950.

No. 46205 *Princess Victoria* was instantly recognisable after 1938, by virtue of its altered valve gear with large 'tripod' motion brackets. These are apparent in this picture taken at Brinklow in 1950. The engine had been renumbered in May 1948 and repainted the following November, in the first iteration of BR lined black with Gill Sans smokebox door number plate, 8ins cream cabside numerals and 10ins BRITISH RAILWAYS lettering on the tender.

'Coronation' 'Pacific' No. 46249 *City of Sheffield* heads north in 1950 at Brinklow. It was built non-streamlined, as shown by the curved front footplate, but with a streamlined tender, although this was de-streamlined in 1945. It is still in LM&SR 1946 lined black, albeit very unkempt, and was renumbered in April 1948, when the scroll pattern numberplate shown here was fitted. No. 46249 was repainted in BR standard blue during September 1950.

'AL6' electric No. E3194 in the snow of January 1969 at Brinklow on a southbound freight, probably the 06.00 Wallerscote Sidings to Sudbury Sidings. The locomotive entered traffic in January 1966 and became No. 86234 under TOPS.

Nuneaton

At Nuneaton Trent Valley the West Coast main line met the L&NWR lines from Wigston, to the south of Leicester, and Coventry. A Midland Railway line ran to Whitacre and Birmingham, and there was a joint Midland/L&NWR line to Shackerstone and the Leicestershire coalfields. An avoiding line allowing direct running from the Leicester to Whitacre lines also complicated the layout and junctions. There was a large running shed to serve the extensive freight workings, including coal trains generated from the local and South Leicestershire collieries. The

shed gained extra duties from the former Midland Railway shed at nearby Stockingford when, in 1932, the LM&SR concentrated all locomotives at the former L&NWR shed. Wartime congestion was so severe in the shed yard that, in 1944, the LM&SR constructed a new access to the shed from the avoiding loop line, dipping under the L&NWR main line and directly onto the turntable road. The standard L&NWR north-light shed, by then dilapidated, was rebuilt in 1957-8 and closed in June 1966, still with an all steam allocation, apart from a few diesel shunters.

Unnamed 'Patriot' 4-6-0 No. 45513 at Nuneaton, probably soon after a Heavy General repair carried out at Crewe from January to March 1949, when it received British Railways lined black livery, having been renumbered on its previous works visit in June 1948. The first coach has an LM&SR style destination board showing the train was from Barrow. No. 45513 was allocated to Preston from October 1947 until transferred to Crewe in January 1950. This picture was taken from the engine shed – the spotters on the bank opposite have chosen a good viewing site. Nuneaton No. 1 Signalbox is visible behind the train and the Coventry line junction in the foreground.

Ivatt '2MT' 2-6-2T No. 41237 comes off the Coventry line, with Nuneaton engine shed on the left. It was one of five of the class – No's 41234-8 – allocated there from new in August/ September 1949. All had moved away by January 1953, to either Chester Northgate or Llandudno Junction, No. 41237 leaving for the latter in August 1952.

'Jubilee' No. 45592 *Indore* heading south past Nuneaton shed on 9th July 1961. It had moved from Bushbury to Carnforth the previous May.

A nice shot of Nuneaton shed on 2nd September 1961, showing the variety of former LM&SR classes which could be found there at this date – unidentified engines in this picture include two Stanier '8F' 2-8-0s, an Ivatt '4MT' 2-6-0 and a Stanier 2-6-0. The Stanier 2-6-2T on the left, No. 40135, was a local engine in its second spell at the shed after four years away at Birkenhead Mollington Street. The 'Jubilee' on the right is No. 45556 *Nova Scotia*, a Crewe North engine from 1954 until withdrawn in 1964. Out of view of the camera on the right of the shed were the coaling plant, ash plant and turntable, where the new wartime access to the shed from the Leicester loop line added an additional access point to it.

Class '2P' 4-4-0 No. 40683, seen in the shed yard on 2nd September 1961, had been withdrawn in March. Interestingly, it had been allocated to Nuneaton from October 1952 to March 1953, although it was based at Watford when taken out of service. Also visible on the left is a 'Patriot', probably No. 45541, with an inevitable Stanier 'Mogul' and '8F' No. 48289 on the right of the picture. The mechanised ash disposal plant to the left of No. 40683 was built in 1936.

'Patriot' No. 45541 *Duke of Sutherland*, seen coming off the turntable on 2nd September 1961, had been transferred to Nuneaton at the end of the previous year. It was subsequently to be stored there from the end of September until withdrawn in June 1962. At this date no less than seven of the unrebuilt engines were allocated to the shed, victims of the introduction of new diesels, which caused the larger London Midland Region passenger types to be cascaded down to lesser duties.

Ivatt '4MT' No. 43001, also photographed at Nuneaton on 2nd September 1961, had been fitted with AWS in August 1960. It has its original tender with the square step, which was a trap for the unwary footplateman. The tender has one of those mysterious bars at the rear of the coal space which were probably fitted to warn against the proximity of overhead wires, although no other class with a similar pattern tender was ever equipped with them. No. 43001 moved to the Midlands shed from Devons Road in October 1957, when that depot was taken over by diesels, and stayed until October 1962 when it went to Bescot.

One of the original BR Sulzer Type '4's, No. D10 *Tryfan*, enters Nuneaton Trent Valley with the 4.50pm Euston to Blackpool on 2nd September 1961. The first ten 'Peaks' enjoyed a brief spell in the limelight of West Coast mainline expresses, until they were all banished to working coal trains from Toton in February 1962. *Tryfan* became No. 44010 under TOPS and lasted until May 1977. It was named after Tryfan ('Three Stones') which, at 3,010 feet high, is the fourteenth highest mountain in Wales. (Robert Darlaston)

Ex L&NWR 'Super D's No's 49377 and 49441 are stabled down the side of Nuneaton shed adjacent to the Coventry line on 2nd September 1961. No. 49377 was a visitor from Bescot and would move north to Edge Hill for its final five months of service in May 1962, but No. 49441 was a local resident, withdrawn from Nuneaton a few weeks later in October. The line that leads to the turntable is in the foreground.

The boys wandering round the shed on 7th October 1962 have already noted 'Jinty' 0-6-0T No. 47653. It had moved to Nuneaton in summer 1961 and was to stay until January 1963.

The first of the Stanier 2-6-0s, No. 42945, is dutifully 'booked' by the three spotters as it comes on shed on 7th October 1962. When it was built in October 1933, No. 42945 caused an upset because it emerged from Crewe Works with a Great Western Railway-style safety valve 'bonnet', the photographic evidence of which was quickly ordered to be destroyed but to no avail since several pictures survived. No. 42945 started life in the North West, at Carlisle and Workington, before moving southwards to various sheds, spending nearly two decades in North Wales. It arrived at Nuneaton in September 1961 and stayed for over three years before it went to Gorton in December 1964. The 2-6-0s were mainly used on fitted freight workings.

No. E3055, seen at Nuneaton in the mid-1960s, was the only one of the first generation LMR electrics to have diamond cross-arm pantographs, instead of the single arm Stone-Faiveley pattern fitted to the other locomotives. It was the last of the 'AL2' Class locomotives built in August 1961 at Beyer, Peacock's Gorton works for AEI (Metropolitan Vickers) and was stored for several months before entering traffic in April 1962. The locomotive suffered severe fire damage in September 1966 at Sandbach while working a Manchester-Cardiff train and was stored for several years at Bury before being officially withdrawn in September 1969. The overhead current was energised to Nuneaton in January 1964 and electrically hauled trains started in March, with thirty weekday trains worked to or from the station.

Atherstone

An '8F' 2-8-0 from Birkenhead, No. 48726, with a train of bogie bolster wagons carrying new flat-bottom rail at Atherstone in 1952.

BR Standard 4-6-2 No. 71000 *Duke of Gloucester* on 12th August 1960 near Atherstone. During its short working life of less than ten years, this engine spent most of its time on the West Coast mainline south of Crewe.

Doncaster built 'AL6' electric No. E3129 at Atherstone on 17th July 1968, with the 7K28 13.35 Corby to Crewe Basford Hall freight. This was hardly the best use of a 3600hp electric locomotive when there were plenty of the earlier electric classes available for these lesser duties. No. E3129 became No. 86205 in June 1973, No. 86503 in September 1988 but reverted to No. 86205 in November 1989.

Polesworth

Crewe North 'Royal Scot' No. 46152 *The King's Dragoon Guardsman* on a Down express at Polesworth in the mid-1950s. This is the engine which permanently swapped identities with the original No. 6100 before Royal Scot went to the United States in 1933.

Baddesley Colliery

Baddesley Colliery was about two miles north west of Atherstone and connected to both the L&NWR and Midland Railway, the latter with a mineral branch from Kingsbury. In 1916, Manning Wardle delivered a new large 0-6-0 saddle tank, No. 1891, with 16ins by 24ins outside cylinders and named *Merevale*. However, subsequently, naming after members of the owning family became favoured and so it was renamed *John Robert*. It worked at Baddesley until sent to Birch Coppice in September 1962, after overhaul at Ansley Workshops.

Running from the West Coast main line in the Trent Valley, the colliery line traversed the A5 trunk road at an ungated crossing. The branch rose about 240ft in a distance just short of two miles – an average gradient of 1 in 47 and with 1 in 23 at its steepest. For this, something powerful was required and Garratt *William Francis*, built in 1937, was the answer. Beyer, Peacock Works No. 6841, it was named after Sir William Francis Dugdale, the son of the founder of the colliery. In appearance, this locomotive was virtually identical to the other three Garratt locomotives supplied by Beyer, Peacock for industrial service in this country. The design was a genuine Garratt, the relatively small size not precluding the full use of the basic principles of the type. The engine was returned to the makers in 1956 for general overhaul but by 1966 was worn out, only handling eighteen wagon rakes compared to sixteen for an Austerity 0-6-0ST. *William Francis* is preserved at Bressingham in Norfolk, arriving there in 1968.

Tamworth Low Level

Tamworth's first station was built in 1839 by the Birmingham & Derby Junction Railway, which was absorbed by the Midland Railway in 1844. It became the High Level station in 1847, when the Trent Valley Railway line from Rugby to Stafford was built, passing beneath it, with a new two storey building being opened which served both levels. Tamworth became one of the most important mail transfer stations in the country, with up to 2,000 mailbags handled every night as seven different Travelling Post Office trains called there. This was the main reason why the station was rebuilt when the Trent Valley line was electrified, and special provision was made for the requirements of the Post Office and the TPO crews who changed there from one mail train to another. During the rebuilding, the bridge carrying the High Level tracks had to be raised by two feet to give sufficient clearance for the overhead catenary and all four platforms, on both levels, were lengthened to take fifteen coach trains. The new station was opened in September 1962.

Rebuilt 'Royal Scot' No. 46159 *The Royal Air Force* waits to depart from Tamworth Low Level on a southbound express in the early 1950s. No. 46159 was unusual in retaining its early crest until withdrawn in 1963. Behind, a freight is passing overhead through the High Level station on the former Midland Railway Burton to Birmingham line. One of the three mail lifts linking the Low and High Level platforms is visible on the left of the picture.

'Coronation' No. 46240 *City of Coventry* speeds the Up 'Royal Scot' through Tamworth in 1959. It was one of only three cities in the class to have a badge of the civic coat of arms above the nameplate. In July 1958, it was painted in crimson lake and lined in the British Railways style orange/black but on its next repaint, in August 1960, it appeared with the more familiar LM&SR style yellow/black lining. The AWS was fitted in May 1959.

No. 46247 *City of Liverpool* sweeps through Tamworth in 1959 with 'The Ulster Express', which ran between Heysham and London, connecting with the ferries to Ireland. The 'Coronation' is in British Railways lined crimson lake applied in July 1959, at the same time as it was fitted with AWS. It had originally been repainted in crimson lake, but with LM&SR style lining in May 1958 and was to revert to this pattern in January 1961. Only twenty LM&SR 'Pacific's were given crimson lake livery, the others which generally worked mainly on overnight duties, remained in the cheaper standard green. On the Down platform the wooden structures which housed the two mail lifts are visible; the one on the Up platform is obscured by the engine's exhaust.

BR Sulzer Type '4' No. D4 *Great Gable* at Tamworth in 1961, near the end of its brief two year spell on the West Coast main line. *Great Gable* is located just north of Scafell Pike and is 2,949 feet high; its impressive outline led to it being chosen as the centre piece in the motif used by the Lake District National Park. The first ten locomotives, No's D1-D10, were all named after prominent British mountains and peaks, resulting in the whole class, including the later examples, being given the nickname 'Peaks'. Along with the other nine Pilot Scheme locomotives in the class, No. D4 was transferred to Toton in early 1962. *Great Gable* became No. 44004 under TOPS in April 1974 and, after withdrawal in 1980, was preserved at the Midland Railway Centre, Butterley.

Stanier '8F' 2-8-0 No. 48350 under the wires on the Down through line, with a northbound train of track section empties in 1963. The 'juice' for the West Coast electrification was switched on down to Tamworth during July. A £200,000 rebuilding at Tamworth had been completed the previous September, primarily to improve the operation of the Royal Mail services. The new station buildings, which can just be seen on the extreme right, incorporated an entrance and booking hall.

'Jubilee' No. 45672 *Anson* with a southbound express on the Up through line at Tamworth in 1963. It was allocated to Rugby between June 1961 and December 1963. The Midland Railway signal box and water tower at the High Level station are visible in the right background. During the rebuilding, the old wooden structures housing the mail lifts were replaced with new brick-built ones, as can be seen in the centre above the 'Jubilee'.

Lichfield Trent Valley

The Trent Valley line was crossed for the second time within less than ten miles at Lichfield, this time by another former London & North Western Railway line. The secondary routes from Walsall and Sutton Coldfield passed overhead en route to joining the ex-Midland Railway Birmingham to Burton line just north of Alrewas.

The first main line diesel in Britain, No. 10000, was built by the LM&SR in 1947 and is seen here heading north through Lichfield with an Up Class 'C' express freight in 1950, still with the original cast steel 'LMS' letters on the lower bodyside. These were removed during a Heavy overhaul completed in March 1951 and replaced by the first version of the standard British Railways emblem.

The English Electric 3,300 hp prototype *Deltic* in 1956 on the northern outskirts of Lichfield, passing Milepost 117 at Netherstowe Lane, watched by a group of spotters who were no doubt intrigued by the stunning pale blue diesel. *Deltic* ran on the West Coast main line from late 1955 until the end of 1958, usually working a regular Euston-Liverpool diagram. In June 1957, its schedule was changed to include an additional round trip between London and Crewe daily, in order to show that English Electric's claims for the intensive running made possible through its low maintenance requirements were valid. *Deltic*'s day began with the 12.37am from Crewe to Euston, followed by the 7.55am from Euston to Liverpool, the 2.10pm back to London and ending with the 7.20pm to Crewe. This produced a total daily mileage of 703, which the locomotive worked for six days each week. In January 1959, it left the London Midland, when the Eastern Region finally got its hands on the prototype of the fleet which they had ordered nearly a year before.

Stanier Class '3' 2-6-2T No. 40087 departs southwards from Lichfield Trent Valley in March 1953. No. 40087 was allocated to Nuneaton shed from January 1953 until withdrawn at the end of 1962. In the background is a water tower on the ex-Midland Railway line to Lichfield City and J.&C.H. Evans & Co. Ltd's Trent Valley Maltings. Brewing had been the most important industry in Lichfield from the late 19th century onwards.

Edge Hill 'Coronation' No. 46251 *City of Nottingham* hurries southbound through Lichfield Trent Valley on 'The Shamrock', from Liverpool to London, in April 1955. It was one of the post-war 'Pacific's and hence was not built with a streamlined casing, having a curved front footplate unlike its de-streamlined classmates. No. 46251 had been repainted from lined black into BR green during a works visit completed two months before this picture was taken. The West Coast main line was only double track at this point, hence the facing point into the platform road which is protected by the trap point just visible in the left foreground. It would be another fifty years and an expenditure of several billions before the whole of the Trent Valley route between Rugby and Stafford was quadrupled.

The horse is oblivious as a crowd of admirers watch 'Princess Royal' No. 46204 *Princess Louise* sweep through Lichfield with the Up 'Merseyside Express' in September 1955. It had been painted in green during an overhaul completed in June 1952 but ended its career in crimson lake, initially with British Railways orange/black lining and then with LM&SR style yellow/black lining.

The horse has moved over towards the High Level line but the spotters are still in place as 'Coronation' No. 46241 *City of Edinburgh* runs through with 'The Ulster Express' from Heysham. It was built with a streamlined casing and had a sloping smokebox until July 1953. No. 42641 ran in British Railways blue until October 1954, when it received green livery, although its condition had become pretty poor within less than a year as this picture shows. A '2P' 4-4-0 is just visible in the High Level platform, probably on a local from Birmingham.

'Patriot' 4-6-0 No. 45507 *Royal Tank Corps* pulls out of Lichfield Trent Valley on 7th July 1956 with a southbound express. It was built at Crewe in 1932 as LM&SR No. 5936, renumbered in July 1934 as No. 5507, becoming BR No. 45507 in October 1948. The 'Patriots' in their unrebuilt form were the first of the former LM&SR passenger classes to become extinct, with *Royal Tank Corps* one of the last four survivors when it was withdrawn in October 1962.

No. 46132 *The King's Regiment (Liverpool)* leans into the curve as it rushes through Lichfield with a northbound express circa 1957. The rebuilt 'Scot' was shedded, appropriately, at Edge Hill from October 1954 until September 1959. To the left of the engine is the curve round to the High Level line whilst behind it is Lichfield No. I signal box and the High Level platforms.

A lone spotter watches one of the Southern Railway designed diesel-electrics working a southbound express in June 1958, as a freight passes over it through the High Level station. No. 10203 had been transferred from the Southern Region in August 1955 and worked on the London Midland until withdrawn in 1963.

Blackpool allocated 'Jubilee' No. 45574 *India* sets off northwards in 1958, past a wonderful line of three double slips into the sidings on the left. The Trent Valley Maltings, demolished in about 1971, was served via the spur off the headshunt, from which a siding diverged through the gate behind the sign. Lichfield No. 2 signal box is on the right, with No. 1 box obscured by No. 45574's exhaust.

Class '5' 4-6-0 No. 45003 piloting a 'Royal Scot' with train W296, the 9.0am Blackpool Central-Euston express in 1959. They are passing Lichfield Trent Valley No. 1 signal box which was situated between the Up and Down main lines. Apparently it used to shake rather a lot as trains passed either side.

Edge Hill 'Princess Royal' No. 46204 *Princess Louise* hurries through Lichfield Trent Valley with a northbound express, probably for Liverpool. The photograph was taken some time after it was fitted with AWS in June 1959. In the left background, the water tower on the High Level line can just be seen.

A small audience watches No. 46208 *Princess Helena Victoria* as it runs through on the 1L28 Saturdays Only 11.45am Euston to Workington express in 1960. The gentleman on the right is obviously not a railway enthusiast, unlike those further down the platform. Note the two permanent way men in the six-foot on the platform line – no hi-visibility jackets in those days!

English Electric Type '4' No. D222 departs northwards from Lichfield Trent Valley in late 1959, long before its naming as *Laconia* in October 1962 and still with the original nose ladder. It entered service in July 1959, was renumbered as No. 40022 in 1974 and remained in service until 1984.

There are lots of interesting points in this picture of Willesden allocated Stanier 2-8-0 No. 48600, passing under the High Level bridge and two as yet unconnected overhead line gantries. The '8F' is paired with one of the ten flat high-sided 3,500 gallon tenders built with 'Jubilees' No's 5607-5616 in 1934, before the standard Stanier tender with turned-in sides was introduced. It had received this tender in place of its 4,000 gallon type during December 1958, in a swap with 'Jubilee' No. 45719. The tank wagons are probably for bitumen and are privately owned, the second one carrying an owner's name on the side board; unusually it has two manholes. There is a gleaming new diesel shunter next to the tender, annoyingly only revealing the first digit of its number. It was possibly one of the batch No's D4131-4133, built in May 1962, on its way down from Horwich to Cricklewood.

Another Willesden '8F', No. 48171, passes through with a northbound Empty Coaching Stock (ECS) train, as the ladies on the Up platform wait for a southbound local. The overhead line gantries and new signals are in place but the power was not switched on until August 1963.

The English Electric Type '4's had taken over most of the regular express work on the West Coast main line by the time this picture was taken in 1962. No. D370 is working north on 'The Midday Scot', a regular Stanier 'Pacific' duty for almost thirty years. It was one of the last of the class built without a yellow warning panel, when it entered service in December 1961; these were introduced from early 1962.

Class 'AL5' electric No. E3059 near Lichfield on 2nd August 1966, with the 3K07 10.52am Euston-Crewe parcels train. It was built at Doncaster Works in July 1961, becoming No. 85004 under TOPS in September 1974 and then No. 85111 in November 1989, when it was converted for use on freight trains, only four months before it was withdrawn following extensive damage to its transformer.

Class 'AL6' electric No. E3185, built by Vulcan Foundry in September 1965, is seen at Whittington, south of Lichfield, on 6th October 1967, with the lengthy 3A26 07.19am Crewe-Euston parcels. The locomotive carried three different TOPS numbers, beginning with No. 86005 in June 1973, followed by No. 86405 in 1986 and No. 86605 in 1990, reverting finally to No. 86405 in 1992.

Rugeley Trent Valley

Rugeley Trent Valley was the third of the closely spaced junction stations on the Trent Valley line. Unlike the two to the south, it had a ground level intersection, with the branch from Walsall via Cannock.

No. 46229 *Duchess of Hamilton* in 1959-60 on 'The Ulster Express' near Rugeley, with the power station in the background. The AWS and LM&SR yellow/black style lining were applied in October 1959. On withdrawal, the locomotive was purchased by Butlins and was exhibited at their Minehead holiday camp, until it was 'rescued' by the National Railway Museum. After restoration to working order in 1989, No. 46229 returned to the main line for seven years until its boiler ticket expired in 1996. Its streamlined casing was restored at Tyseley Locomotive Works between 2005 and 2009, and *Duchess of Hamilton* is currently a static exhibit at York.

A Park Royal two-car diesel multiple unit stands at the west side of Rugeley Trent Valley station in 1961, after arrival from Walsall. The unit, which became TOPS Class '103', was allocated to Ryecroft and has '3C' stencilled on both corners of the bufferbeam. Two nattily dressed workman are walking alongside the Engineer's train. In the centre background, above the recently erected overhead gantry, can be seen part of the Grade 2 listed Colton Mill Bridge, spanning the River Trent.

Immaculate No. DP2 passes through Rugeley with either the 1A40 2.05pm SX or 2.10pm SO Liverpool to Euston express in 1962. The English Electric owned 2,700bhp prototype ran on the London Midland Region from May 1962 until mid-1963. It was built as 'Deltic' construction at Vulcan Foundry was drawing to a close and utilised a 'Deltic' style body shell, although with greatly different engine and traction equipment. While on the London Midland, No. DP2 successfully worked an intensive six days a week cyclic diagram between London Euston and Liverpool and, from May 1963, Blackpool. In June 1963, it was moved to Finsbury Park and was allocated to the 'Deltic' pool, where it worked turn and turn about with its more powerful brethren. Its career came to an abrupt end in a collision at Thirsk in July 1967 but not before it had led to an order for fifty locomotives of what soon became Class '50'. Unfortunately, the excellent and well-proven design of the prototype was ruined by the addition of several untried features.

Stafford

The Trent Valley line from Rugby met the Grand Junction line from Birmingham and Wolverhampton, opened in 1837, just to the south of Stafford station. At the north end, the Shropshire Railways & Canal Company opened its line from Wellington to Stafford in 1849, which it had leased to the L&NWR even before it was opened. This was followed in 1867 by the Stafford & Uttoxeter Railway, later to become an outpost of the Great Northern Railway, with its line from Broomhall Junction, north of Uttoxeter, on the North Staffordshire Railway line from Stoke to Derby. Although the latter closed as a through line in 1951, having lost its passenger service in 1939, and the Wellington line would follow in September 1964, Stafford remained an important junction between the two main lines from the south and hence was completely rebuilt as part of the West Coast main line electrification. The track layout was rationalised with the main line platforms removed and a new island platform built to serve the Stoke line; the new station was officially opened in December 1962.

Midland Railway built '2P' 4-4-0 No. 40332 bagged up and stored out of use on Stafford shed. A Crewe North engine, it was in store there from February to September 1956. This was not the end of its working life, however, because it was transferred to Bristol Barrow Road in March 1957, where it lasted until September 1959, having been joined by classmate No. 40501.

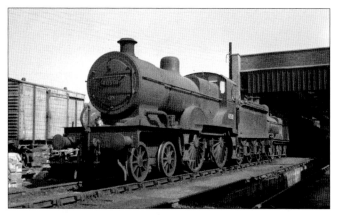

Ryecroft Class '2P' 4-4-0 No. 40501, seen at Stafford shed in 1956, went to Bristol Barrow Road in December 1957.

No. 46255 *City of Hereford* heads north from Stafford in 1955 with the fourteen coaches of 'The Mid-Day Scot'. It was the last of the 'standard' Stanier 'Coronations', entering traffic in October 1946. It was in BR express blue livery until January 1953, when it was given the green livery which it kept until withdrawal in September 1964. The train is passing the extensive timber yard of Henry Venables Ltd, a firm founded around 1860, which was based on this site until about 2000. The company built up an extensive business supplying specialist timber products and was involved in a number of high profile projects, including the restoration of York Minster after fire, the construction of the Lantern Lobby at Windsor Castle, the building of the Globe Theatre at Southwark and the Swan Theatre in Stratford-upon-Avon.

No. 46254 *City of Stoke-on-Trent* arriving at Stafford from the north. The picture was taken between the fitting of AWS equipment in October 1959 and its repainting in crimson lake with LM&SR yellow/black lining in June 1960, in place of the British Railways orange/black version. The six spotters perched on the wall and the posters on the end of the terrace advertising 'Butlers Bitter - Pride of the Midlands' and 'Belle Vue Zoo and Gardens' are typical of the period; another group is peering from the road overbridge. Stafford No. 5 signal box and the entrance to the shed yard are on the left.

Taken from just beyond the overbridge in the previous photograph, English Electric Type '4' No. D313 on the Up Fast in the early 1960s, passing the erecting shop of the Castle Works of W.G. Bagnall Limited, self-proclaimed 'Builders of Locomotives for the World's Railways'. It was one of the smaller British locomotive manufacturers, building mostly industrial locomotives, although it did produce some 'Jinties' for the LM&SR in the late 1920s and some '94xx' "Pannier" tanks for the Western Region in the early 1950s. The turnout and crossover in front of the Type '4' are for the junction with the ex-Great Northern Railway line to Uttoxeter, which can be seen curving off to the right. This closed as a through route on 5th March 1951, although a stub survived to serve the RAF Stafford 16 Maintenance Unit depot, closing in December 1975.

The English Electric Type '4's took over haulage of the principal West Coast main line expresses from 1959 onwards. No. D333 heads 'The Caledonian' on the Up Fast as it passes the Bagnall Works. The Anglo-Scottish express was introduced in June 1957, running with a then very light loading of just eight coaches, enabling it to reach Glasgow in 6 hours 40 minutes. The front of the train is passing over the junction – off to the left – for the line to Wellington and Shrewsbury, which passed between Bagnall's erecting shop and the works of the Universal Grinding Wheel Company; a 'Jinty' can just be seen above the roof of the diesel.

No. 46209 *Princess Beatrice* passing through the remains of the L&NWR station, with electrification work well under way. The fireman has moved across the footplate to join the driver in posing for the cameras. The picture was taken after the 'Princess' was fitted with AWS in May 1959, probably during 1960 while it was allocated to Crewe North. It was equipped with a Smith-Stone speed recorder in December 1957.

'Coronation' No. 46224 *Princess Alexandra* at Stafford, in a picture taken after January 1961 when it received its AWS equipment. No. 46224 was based at Polmadie shed in Glasgow from 1939 until withdrawn in October 1963. The gantries for the electrification are now in place but work was not completed and the current switched on until late 1962.

The new station is taking shape in the background as Crewe North 'Royal Scot' No. 46148 *The Manchester Regiment*, on the Up through road, passes Fairburn '4MT' 2-6-4T No. 42267 in the bay. The power of the rebuilt 'Scots' was used to the full on the long expresses of the West Coast main line, particularly given the relatively small number of 'Pacific's available.

Stanier '8F' No. 48723 on the Up platform line, with Stafford No. 4 Signal Box visible under the bridge and a 'blood & custard' liveried Commer lorry parked in front. The Crewe South 2-8-0 received 'Old Standard' 3,500 gallon riveted tender No. 4496 from 'Jubilee' No. 45587 in May 1960, after being paired for most of its life with a Stanier 4,000 gallon type. Behind the tender is a shock absorbing open wagon fitted with a tarpaulin bar.

'Royal Scot' No. 46169 *The Boy Scout* speeds under the newly installed overhead wires with a northbound express. This was the last engine in the class, built at Derby in 1930. It had been transferred from Crewe North to Willesden in April 1962, which narrows down the date of this photograph to the middle of that year. The early LM&SR van on the left has been fitted with stepboards and is prominently labelled 'EM Walsall - Relaying Gang Tool Van'.

Fairburn '4MT' 2-6-4T No. 42183 at Stafford with the 4.01pm local to Wellington via Newport (Salop) on 9th November 1962, with the new station almost complete. It had been transferred to Crewe North from Northampton the previous month but was to stay there for just three months, going to Rugby in January 1963. (Robert Darlaston)

The length and bulk of the BR Sulzer 'Peak' Type '4' is emphasised in this picture of No. D1 *Scafell Pike*, watched by three young trainspotters dressed in a fashion which really dates the picture. The name given to the first of what would become later become Class '44' was that of England's highest peak, at 3,210 feet, which is located at the southern end of the Lake District. No. D1 officially entered traffic in August 1959 and, after spending some time at Derby, moved to Camden in April 1960 and on to Longsight the next month. One working associated with the class on the West Coast main line was the 7.45am Crewe-Euston, and they would also be frequently found on the Euston-Blackpool and Crewe-Perth workings. No. D1 caught fire on 29th September 1961 near Kings Langley, while working the 8.15am Manchester-Euston and was quickly despatched to Derby Works. It moved to Toton in early 1962, as the first ten 'Peaks' were concentrated there for freight work, and became No. 44001 in February 1974, before it was withdrawn in October 1976.

2 – Rugby to Coventry and Birmingham

Historically, the London Midland route to Birmingham was the first to be finished, when the London & Birmingham Railway reached the city in 1838, whilst the Western Region line, in its final form via High Wycombe and Banbury, was not completed until 1910. Coventry was the only significant station on the line between Rugby and Birmingham and, like New Street, was to be completely rebuilt when the line was electrified in the 1960s. The route to some extent played second fiddle to the Trent Valley line, especially in terms of motive power. The Stanier 'Pacific's did not work into the West Midlands until the late 1950s, after they had been displaced by diesels on the West Coast main line and the principal expresses were for many years worked by 'Patriot' and 'Jubilee' 4-6-0s, supplemented in later years by 'Royal Scots'. English Electric Type '4' diesels appeared briefly in the early 1960s, until the electrics took over in 1967 with a significantly improved hourly service which soon became even more frequent.

Foleshill

A 'G2' Class 0-8-0 chugs through Foleshill in 1959, on a freight from the Nuneaton direction, as a lady and her children wait for the next local to Coventry. Foleshill is a suburb about three miles north east of the city centre, and the station and the adjacent ones at Coundon Road and Daimler Halt were used extensively in the mornings and evenings by factory workers up until the late 1950s, with long corrugated iron waiting shelters provided on both platforms for them. The footbridge which frames the train was built in 1931 from London & North Western Railway parts.

Nominally independent, the Foleshill Railway was opened in 1901 to serve Webster's Brickworks from a junction off the Coventry to Nuneaton line. In 1905, it was extended to serve the new Courtaulds factory and Coventry Ordnance Works. During the First World War, the line carried much heavy ordnance traffic from the Admiralty works, some of which was in the form of gun barrels for the Royal Navy's 'Dreadnought' Class battleships. The Ordnance Works alone dispatched 40,000 tons of traffic and the Foleshill Munitions Factory was responsible for another 232,500 tons of wartime traffic. The works was also connected to the Coventry loop line, which in later days carried the majority of the traffic. Coventry Ordnance Co. was acquired by the Admiralty in about 1936 and re-equipped. Andrew Barclay Works No. 2053 of 1938 was part of that refurbishment programme. Originally named *Coventry*, it was also known as *Nellie*, which name was painted above the original nameplates, as can be seen in this photograph taken at the Admiralty Stores Depot on 3rd March 1962; it was scrapped soon after.

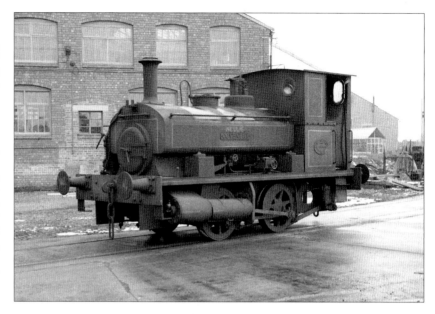

Ruston & Hornsby supplied this 0-4-0 diesel, Works No. 284844, in 1950 and it became West Midlands Gas Board No. 5 at Foleshill. It is seen here in fully lined livery with the feint outline 'Nº 5' just visible at the top centre of the bonnet. After rail traffic at the site ceased in March 1969, the diesel ended up with Birds at Long Marston in 1972 but was fortunate not to be scrapped, instead being exported to Belgium the following year.

Coventry Corporation Gas Works, built in 1909 between Longford & Exhall and Foleshill stations, was situated in pleasant green fields. W. Bagnall Works No. 2286 of 1925 was one of a fleet of four Bagnall locomotives supplied for use here. They were all to be scrapped on site by Sheppards' (Coals & Metals), one each year from 1962 to 1965, with No. 2286 being the last, surviving to July 1965.

Coventry

Coventry station opened to passenger services in 1838 but was altered many times over the next seventy years, although the basic layout with four lines through the station remained unchanged. It was due to be improved in the mid-1930s but the outbreak of the Second World War curtailed this. By the 1950s, the whole station could at best be described as ramshackle, with parts of the original 1838 buildings still in use in 1959. This hardly suited the dynamic image the city was attempting to portray and so the decision to totally rebuild the station was warmly welcomed. Work started in 1959 and was completed in 1962.

Ex-LM&SR 'Compound' 4-4-0 No. 41172 is seen standing at Coventry's Platform 2 on 8th June 1952, with the 1.43pm Coventry to Birmingham New Street service. Built by the Vulcan Foundry in November 1925, No. 41172 remained in service until July 1957, when it was withdrawn from Rugby shed. To the right of the locomotive at the end of the Down platform can be seen the London & Birmingham Railway water column, which is now at the National Railway Museum, and wagons standing on the spur to the L&BR shed. To the rear of the water crane was the 'incline machine', a timber framed and clad structure built on steel girders, dating back to 1901-4, which was used to handle large crowds of passengers arriving back from their holiday excursions. It was open above waist level and there was a dog-leg half way up the ramp, where it turned ninety degrees on the level and then it continued to the exit located on Warwick Road.

One of the three North British diesel hydraulic 0-4-0s allocated from new in 1958 to Rugby, No. D2910. It is seen here on Saturday 27th June 1959 at 8.15pm, shunting parcels vehicles at the west end of Coventry station. *The Railway Observer* reported that '*One of them now takes the weekly shunting duty at Coventry, replacing a 350 hp diesel. The two diesel shunters (a NBL 300 hp and a BR 350 hp) are serviced at Rugby every two weeks; they stay in the goods yard overnight. The 350 hp shunter also acts as station pilot in the evening.*' The signalman at the top of the steps of Coventry No. 2 signal box is having a chat. (Michael Mensing)

Class '5' No. 45284 is shrouded in steam on 18th November 1960, with evidence in the background that the rebuilding of Coventry station had started. This engine was allocated to Rugby for just three weeks, transferring from Willesden at the end of October 1960 and returning there in the week this picture was taken.

Rebuilding is now well underway at Coventry station on 29th July 1961, as Fairburn Class '4MT' 2-6-4T No. 42267 calls with the 8.50am Birmingham New Street-Peterborough East train. The DMU on the left is probably working a Leamington to Nuneaton service. (Robert Darlaston)

North British diesel-hydraulic 0-4-0 No. D2911 at the new Platform 4 on 13th June 1961, as the railway staff play 'pass the parcel'. They were filling the open wagon in order to transfer parcels to the Up side of the station during the rebuilding, because the main overbridge had been taken out of use. (Michael Mensing)

A Metropolitan-Cammell two-car DMU on a Leamington Spa working in 1962, just after the new Coventry station had been officially opened on 30th April. The clean lines of the new buildings would not be spoilt for a few years, until the overhead wires of the London Midland electrification were extended through the West Midlands in 1966-7.

Colliery engines

The Warwickshire Coal Company developed Keresley Colliery from 1902, although sinking was not completed until 1919. The colliery was connected to the Coventry-Nuneaton line by a two mile long private railway. Peckett Works No. 1745 of 1927 was named *Coventry No. 4* and worked there until it was sent to Andrew Barclays for refurbishment in 1963. Afterwards it went to Arley Colliery but returned to Kerseley in September 1968 and was scrapped on site by T.W. Ward a year later.

Three of the ten Western Region '15xx' Class 'Pannier' tanks were sold to the National Coal Board in 1961 and, after refurbishment at Andrew Barclay, were used at Coventry Colliery from the summer of 1962, with No. 1509 not arriving until March 1963. The Hawksworth designed engines, introduced in 1949, were the last in a long line of Great Western "Pannier"s and one of only two classes with outside cylinders, the other being the '1366' class. They were best known for their work on empty stock duties at Paddington. No. 1509, pictured at the colliery in 1969, along with No. 1502 survived until 1970 and they were then used as a source of spare parts for the third engine, No. 1501, which was preserved and is to be found today working on the Severn Valley Railway. No. 1509 was not so fortunate and was scrapped by John Cashmore Ltd at Great Bridge in October 1970.

Stechford

Fronting the Birmingham Outer Ring Road (the A4040) and located at the junction of the main line from Euston to Birmingham New Street and the direct (avoiding) line to Aston, Stechford was relatively busy with passenger and freight traffic. The Down platform had a water crane at the Birmingham end and the No. 2 signal box was separated from the platform by the exit road from the Down loop. The junction with the Aston line was some 150 yards after the signal box. The Up platform gave a good view of the Up goods yard, which differed from the Down yard in that very little shunting was done, except that needed to serve Cartwright & Co. (Timber Merchants & Importers), the coal yard and the common user dock. The yard was also used to drop off single or small rakes of pre-sorted wagons to be picked up by other trains and it was common to have rakes of engineers wagons in the yard for lengthy periods of time.

Immediately before the station on the Down side was a nine road sorting sidings yard which was gravity worked. Goods trains also used the Down passenger loop, often taking on water on arrival and then waiting clearance to pull forward onto the main, or Aston line. This was in order to bring the rear of the train clear of the points, allowing them to reverse and shunt their train over the hump located immediately to the east of the A4040 bridge. In the event of conflicting traffic, which was quite common, the train would pull right forward onto the Aston line (often with a local spotter in the cab) and then, after the traffic had cleared, reverse back into the loop shunting the train as it passed slowly over the hump. The No. 1 signal box overlooked the Down marshalling yard from its position on the other side of the main line.

Contrasting the old and the new at Stechford on 18th November 1967. Upper is the decaying wooden former L&NWR booking hall and station office, which was located above the main running lines between Birmingham and Coventry at the Up end of the platforms. The second picture shows the uninspiring new brick-clad booking hall which replaced it, approached from Victoria Road. (Robert Darlaston)

Bushbury 'Jubilee' No. 45738 *Samson* roars through Stechford on the Up Main with 'The Midlander' to Euston in 1955. This Restaurant car express was introduced in October 1950 and was the fastest steam-hauled service between the first and second cities, taking a little over two hours at its best in 1958, which was over thirty minutes less than in 1950. On the left behind the water tower is Stechford No. 2 signal box and on the right in the background are the Up sidings.

Stanier '4MT' 2-6-4T No. 42541 at Stechford with a Coventry City football special to the Aston Villa FC ground at Witton, signalled to take the direct line to Aston, on 31st October 1959. (Coventry lost to Aston Villa – in fact it would be almost forty years until they next won against them, in 1998). Stechford's extensive Up sidings are on the right. Note that, since 1955, electric station lamps had been fitted at this suburban location, at a time when some of those at New Street were still gas powered. (Robert Darlaston)

Bushbury 'Jubilees' worked the London to West Midlands expresses for about twenty-five years, although they had an inauspicious start when first introduced because of severe problems with their early low-superheat boilers. No. 45742 *Connaught* is passing Stechford No. 2 signal box with the 8.30 am Euston to Wolverhampton High Level on 21st April 1959. Part of the terrace of L&NWR railwaymen's cottages are just visible on the left behind the goods yard. (Robert Darlaston)

Southern Railway designed diesel-electric No. 10203 approaches Stechford with the final working of the 2.30pm Birmingham New Street to Euston service, the 1.48pm from Wolverhampton High Level, on Saturday, 31st October 1959. From 2nd November, all express services between London and Birmingham used the former Great Western line from Snow Hill to Paddington during electrification of the London Midland route. The fencing visible on the left is around a private preparatory school's small playing field. (Robert Darlaston)

Stanier 'Princess' 4-6-2 No. 46200 *The Princess Royal*, leaking steam badly, approaches Stechford with the Up 'Ulster Express' on Sunday, 30th October 1960. The train had been diverted from its usual route on the Trent Valley line between Rugby and Stafford because of electrification works. (Robert Darlaston)

Unrebuilt 'Patriot' No. 45533 *Lord Rathmore* passes Stechford with another diverted Trent Valley main line working, a Down empty stock train on Sunday 30th October 1960. (Robert Darlaston)

Aston

The pioneer main line diesel No. 10000 in the mid-1950s in BR black with the cycling lion emblem. The location is the avoiding line between Aston and Stechford stations, where the line runs alongside Aston Church Road. This photograph was taken from Warren Road bridge looking towards Aston. This scene changed considerably around 1959-60, when a number of small self-contained yards appeared alongside the line.

BR Sulzer Type '2' No. D5082 approaches Aston station on a northbound express freight coming off the Windsor Street Goods lines in May 1962, shortly before it was transferred from Willesden to Watford. The diesel entered service in March 1960, was renumbered as No. 24082 in October 1973 and was withdrawn in 1979. The train was a forerunner of what would become the northbound 'Condor'. As well as the better known London to Scotland service, the 'Condor' (name derived from CONtainer DOoR-to-Door) was also used for the fast overnight freight service from Aston to Glasgow, introduced on 17th January 1963.

Stanier '8F' No. 48752 just next to Aston shed, coming from Stechford on the Down line on 24th May 1964. It had acquired an ex-'Jubilee' 3,500 gallon snap head riveted tender in December 1958, in place of its original 4,000 gallon Stanier tender. The train is intriguing, a 'Lowmac' sandwiched between two brake vans and we wonder if it has anything to do with the rather large pipe above the tracks which is being installed. Work on this has not finished because there are no 'anti-climb' protectors fitted; these were required even in 1964.

Aston shed

The ex-L&NWR shed at Aston was located in the 'V' of the lines to Stechford and New Street, close to Aston station. The twelve road shed was built in 1883 to the company's standard design. Its engines were mainly employed on freight services, Bushbury shed at Wolverhampton providing the motive power for the London expresses. It was modernised in the 1930s, when mechanical coaling and ash disposal equipment was installed,

together with a 60 foot turntable. Aston was re-coded from 3D to 21D in May 1960 and then became 2J in September 1963 until closure in October 1965. Aston was very difficult to 'bunk', as the only way in, without crossing running lines, was through a door in the shed wall which opened onto a flight of stone steps leading down to a point by the foreman's office and the locomotive disposal board.

The evening shift at Aston coal up Crewe North 'Jubilee' No. 45643 *Rodney* on 18th February 1962. The locals must have loved the sounds of the coaler!

One of Aston's own Stanier '8F' 2-8-0s, No. 48718, being coaled up from the crane on 7th April 1963, presumably because there was a problem with the large tower. No. 48718 was built for the L&NER at the Southern Railway's Brighton Works in August 1944, one of ninety-three constructed there during World War Two. It carried three different numbers before it became No. 8718 in November 1947, starting with No. 7664 when built, No. 3113 in April 1946 and No. 3513 in March 1947. Note the sign 'BR Engines must not pass this Board' – this applied to the road on which the wagon was standing, the '8F' has not violated it.

3 – Burton to Birmingham

The former Midland Railway main line from Derby to Birmingham was opened by the Birmingham & Derby Junction Railway in 1839, originally intending to reach the city by a connection with the London & Birmingham Railway at Stechford. However the need for its own line quickly became apparent and a new direct route was opened in 1842 from Whitacre to Lawley Street via Water Orton and Castle Bromwich. The Birmingham & Derby merged with the Midland Counties Railway and the North Midland Railway to form the Midland Railway in 1844 and ten years later transferred its Birmingham station to the L&NWR's New Street station. A final change to the route was the building of a short cut between Water Orton and Kingsbury which was used primarily by passenger traffic although fast fitted goods were also allowed access at certain times of the day.

The line from Burton ran through a generally rural setting until it reached Tamworth where it crossed over the West Coast main line at what became an important interchange for postal traffic. At the Birmingham end, the building

of a large marshalling yard was started in 1877 at Washwood Heath, and what became known as the Down Siding was built between Bromford Bridge and Saltley, where the Midland had built its principal Birmingham engine shed. The Kingsbury Branch was a most important source of traffic, despite being single line, as it served several collieries.

An interesting legacy from the early days which continued well after nationalisation was the Midland Railway designation of trains as starting from Derby, which meant those travelling to Birmingham were classified as Down and those going to Derby as Up trains, This was the opposite to all other railways in Britain where northbound services would be classified as Down and vice versa, because that was determined by whether the train was going towards or away from London.

'Austerity' 2-8-0 No. 90243, from Royston shed, with a Down Class 'H' through freight passing over Haselour water troughs north of Tamworth. The train is heading for Birmingham, probably to Washwood Heath sidings. In the background is Syerscote Lane bridge and, on the right, the water tank supplying the troughs.

A Stanier '8F' 2-8-0 No. 48653 with a Down Class 'H' through freight on Haselour water troughs, just north of the High Level station; these were also known as Wiggington troughs. The '8F' has '16D' painted below its shedplate, which indicates that this picture was taken between September 1963, when its shed was re-coded from 16A, and August 1964 when it was transferred to Derby; presumably the new code had been painted on until the new shedplate was fixed.

In October 1962, No. 92028 was transferred from Kettering to Saltley and the painted '2E' shedcode shows it was photographed around the time the shed was re-coded '2E' in September 1963, and before the engine moved to Birkenhead in November. The former Crosti-boilered 2-10-0 had been converted to a conventional boiler at Crewe Works in late 1959. This Down coal train is running with Class 'H' headlamp code 'Through Freight or Ballast Train', probably to Washwood Heath Sidings.

No. 92137 in the early 1960s on a Down Class 'D' express freight again passing over the water troughs just north of Tamworth High Level station, heading for Birmingham. The '9F' was allocated to Saltley from new in June 1957 and stayed there until moving to Croes Newydd in late 1966.

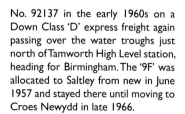

Burton-based 'Crab' 2-6-0 No. 42855 on a Down parcels in 1961, approaching Haselour troughs.

BR Standard Class '5' No. 73136 near Tamworth High Level in 1961, with a northbound 'Express freight with not less than one third of the vehicles fitted' train, which has just come off the water troughs and is about to pass under Syerscote Lane bridge at Wiggington. The piece of agricultural machinery on the left is interesting; it looks to be a potato harvester but is unusual for this period in having the tractor unit combined with it.

Tamworth High Level

This was Tamworth's first station, built in 1839 by the Birmingham & Derby Junction Railway, which was absorbed by the Midland Railway in 1844. It became the High Level station in 1847 when the Trent Valley Railway line from Rugby to Stafford was built, passing beneath it, and a new two storey building was opened which served both levels. Although it lacked the glamour of the West Coast line below with its Stanier 'Pacific's, the High Level station saw both a significant flow of freight traffic between the Midlands and the northern industrial towns and cities as well as the cross-country expresses from the south west to the north east. Tamworth was also one of the most important Royal Mail transfer stations in the country with three lift shafts connecting the High and Low Level platforms to deal with the transfer of the large volume of mail handled every night.

Stanier '8F' No. 48153 from Derby shed runs through Tamworth High Level on a southbound Class 'J' mineral or empty wagon train.

Class '9F' 2-10-0 No. 92053 pounds through the station with a Class 'H' freight headed for Birmingham. The picture was taken while it was shedded at Wellingborough, between November 1959 and September 1962, when it moved to Toton. All three of the mail lifts are visible in this picture. The one on the left is for the Down line below and the one just visible in the centre above the chimney of the '9F' is also for the Down line; the third one on the right is to the Up platform. The main postal traffic flows were between the northbound Bristol-Birmingham-Derby route and the West Coast main line and vice versa; the flows between the southbound Trent Valley line and northbound from Bristol to Derby (and vice versa) were smaller.

Saltley-based Class '5' No. 44814 passing the strangely titled Perrin & Harrisons Siding signal box near Wilnecote, on the southern edge of Tamworth, with a Class 'C' mixed parcels train in 1962.

No. 45650 *Blake* near Perrin & Harrisons siding at Wilnecote in 1962. It was one of the eighteen 'Jubilees' transferred to Burton in late 1961, the biggest single reallocation to one shed for the class and is running under Class 'H' 'Through Freight or Ballast train' headlamps. The 8Z02 so beautifully chalked on the smokebox indicating a special freight from the Eastern Region was probably applicable to a previous train.

Whitacre, Water Orton and Hams Hall

The first Whitacre station was opened in 1842 by the Birmingham & Derby Junction Railway on its new direct line to Birmingham. When the line between Birmingham and Nuneaton was opened in November 1864, the original station was replaced by a new station three-quarters of a mile to its south, at the junction with the new line. The Midland ran trains through to Leicester using running powers over the L&NWR line from Nuneaton and, for most of the years between 1910 and the late 1950s, the Nuneaton line enjoyed a service of between thirteen and sixteen trains each day. Diesel Multiple Units were introduced in 1962 but all the intermediate stations between New Street and Nuneaton, except Water Orton but including Whitacre, were closed in March 1968. Water Orton station was also opened in 1842 as one of the four intermediate stations between Whitacre and Lawley Street. It was later re-sited to the west of its original location. The Midland Railway, which was formed in 1844 when the Birmingham &

Derby Junction Railway, the North Midland Railway and the Midland Counties Railway amalgamated, built a short cut-off line avoiding Whitacre, running from Kingsbury to a new junction at Water Orton, which opened in 1909. This line was designated as the Fast Line while the one via Whitacre and Coleshill was the Slow Line.

Stanier Class '5' No. 44858 arriving at Whitacre with the 6.25pm Birmingham New Street to Derby local on 30th August 1961. (Robert Darlaston)

Water Orton

Saltley '3F' 0-6-0 No. 3812 approaching Water Orton on the Down Slow lines via Whitacre Junction in the summer of 1949. It would be renumbered in October of that year. Note the broken buffer head, an unusual sight but no doubt continuing austerity conditions meant it was not a high priority for changing. No. 43812 would stay allocated to Saltley for all of its remaining years, being withdrawn in June 1961.

No. 43506, a former Midland Railway Class '3F' 0-6-0 from Gloucester shed, at Water Orton on a northbound Class 'H' through freight train of coal empties in 1949. Note the early use of flat bottom rail, whilst it looks as if the Down line has had its ballast cleared out ready for renewal. The '3F' is passing signal No. 50 on the direct, or Fast lines, with the bracket 12/10 in the background; the supplementary arm 16 is not visible in the murk. The track circuit diamond is correctly fitted on signal 50.

Beyer-Garratt No. 47989 with a heavy Toton to Washwood Heath Class 'J' through mineral coal train on 7th January 1951. The train has taken what were known as the Slow Lines via Whitacre Junction and, having joined the Leicester line, is approaching Water Orton. From March 1950, Garratts from Toton had begun working through to Westerleigh sidings near Bristol on an evening mineral train. Previously, they had rarely penetrated west of Birmingham, usually only as far as Kings Norton, to return light engine immediately afterwards.

Beyer-Garratt No. 47981 and an '8F' 2-8-0 leave Water Orton and head for Tamworth and probably Toton on the direct or Fast lines in 1951. Note that in comparison with the bottom photograph on the opposite page, the Down line has now been relaid with flat bottom rail.

Former L&NWR 0-8-0 No. 49430 in the early 1950s, on the Up Slow line approaching Water Orton with an unfitted Class 'H' freight. The 'G2' had been transferred to Nuneaton shed in autumn 1951 and stayed there until September 1960, when it moved to Bescot. There were at least two Nuneaton '7F's booked to visit Washwood Heath during the day on Targets 80 and 84. No. 49430 was one of four 'G2s' to survive at Bescot until 1964 and one of the regular duties for them was from Bescot Yard to Washwood Heath, thence Water Orton to Wolverhampton, back to Aldridge and then light engine back to Bescot.

Fairburn 2-6-4T No. 42186 on an 'Ordinary Passenger Train' in the 1950s at Water Orton. It has just left the station and is heading for Whitacre Junction and Nuneaton, probably on a Leicester service. No. 42186 was shedded at Bournville from new in February 1949 until January 1959, when it was transferred to Hasland.

Ivatt '4MT' No. 43045 with a Leicester to Birmingham passenger train approaching Water Orton station on 3rd March 1951. The 2-6-0 was allocated to Leicester from new on 10th October 1949 until 1958, when it moved to Lancaster.

Class 'B1' 4-6-0 No. 61204 near Water Orton on a Cleethorpes to Birmingham express in 1950, a regular working with an Immingham 'B1'. This particular engine had gone there from new in June 1947. No. 61204 was one of the locomotives transferred to Departmental Stock in December 1963 for use as a stationary boiler for train heating purposes, becoming Departmental No. 19. The drawhook was removed to preclude its use as a normal engine. It lasted in departmental service until March 1966, before being broken up by R.A. Kings of Norwich.

Compound' 4-4-0 No. 41194 on a Birmingham to Leicester 'Ordinary Passenger Train' at Water Orton in late 1952 or early 1953. It had been transferred to Bournville from Southport in October 1952 and was withdrawn from there in 1957. Once again, there is a goods train in the Down lie-by but, since 1949, the wooden buffer stop had been replaced by a rail-built version, probably due to an accident.

'Jubilee' No. 45668 *Madden* running under 'Express Passenger Train' headlamp code, approaching Water Orton on the Down Fast from Tamworth, with Hams Hall Power Station in background. This picture was taken after No. 45668 had moved to Derby in late 1959 but before it was one of the large group of the class transferred to Burton in November 1961.

Hams Hall

Hams Hall was a coal-fired power station situated just to the east of Water Orton, between the Kingsbury and Whitacre lines, and was developed in stages during the middle of the 20th century. Hams Hall 'A' was built in 1929, Hams Hall 'B' opened in 1942 and Hams Hall 'C' in 1958. The three stations were closed over the period from 1975 to 1992 and the site now houses a large industrial park.

As seen in the photograph of No. 45668, Hams Hall had a large CEGB generating station. Situated in a spacious site between the Water Orton to Tamworth and Water Orton to Whitacre Junction lines, it was built in 1929. The station was quoted as burning approximately 774,000 tonnes of coal a year – much of it pulverised coal and all of it coming by rail. Here, a fleet of powerful 18ins 0-6-0Ts provided by Robert Stephenson & Hawthorn were employed up to the mid-1970s. No. 9, Works No. 7151 of 1944, is seen on 14th May 1958, with the cooling towers of Hams Hall 'B' in the background.

Castle Bromwich

No. 44744 passing through Castle Bromwich in July 1955, on a northbound express which appears to consist of all British Railways Mark 1 stock, apart from an ex-L&NER 'strengthener' at the front. The Caprotti Class '5' had recently returned to Bristol Barrow Road after over two years at Leeds Holbeck.

Saltley Class '5' No. 44664 pilots a Thompson 'B1' on a northbound express through Castle Bromwich in 1957. It arrived at the Birmingham shed from Sheffield Millhouses in March 1954 and remained there until transferred to Nottingham in June 1959. No. 44664 was one of the British Railways built engines, delivered from Crewe Works in July 1949, and had all of the post-war modifications, including the forward top feed boiler and self-cleaning smokebox which are evident in this picture. The train is likely to be the returning 'Cleethorpes'.

Three of the two-car Metro-Cammell 'Lightweight' diesel multiple units, newly built at the nearby Washwood Heath factory, arriving at Castle Bromwich in April 1956, on a special working to the British Industries Fair. Twenty-nine of these units went to East Anglia and another seven sets were used by the London Midland Region on the Bury-Bacup line. The three pictured here had Eastern Region numbers and were no doubt being used to help promote the manufacturer during the trade fair.

The sets after arrival at Castle Bromwich station, with its multi-lingual 'Alight here for the Fair' sign. Their 'yellow diamond' couplings made the 'Metro-Cams' compatible only with the Derby 'Lightweights' and Cravens parcels units and this led to their early withdrawal at the end of the 1960s.

The former Southern Region 1-Co-Co-1 No. 10203 was still the most modern mainline diesel electric owned by British Railways in 1957, when it was photographed at Castle Bromwich with a special to the British Industries Fair. It was the forerunner of the English Electric Type '4', later Class '40', having an earlier incarnation of the 2,000bhp 16-cylinder engine, and shared the same length and bulk, weighing in at 132 tons.

Bromford Bridge and Fort Dunlop

Bromford Bridge was built on the site of the original Birmingham & Derby Railway Bromford Forge station, which had only a short life because of the lack of traffic from the surrounding area. It is difficult to believe in this day and age that it was in a very rural area consisting largely of green fields with few villages of consequence. This rural environment was, however, perfect for the creation of Birmingham's race course, which resulted in the new station of Bromford Bridge being built at the extremes of Washwood Heath in 1896. The station never

boasted much in the way of facilities, being similar in operation to other racecourse specific stations throughout the country, in that it was used only on race meeting days. The relatively large signal box, which was a dominant feature of the station, built on the Down platform, was installed to control the approaches to Washwood Heath. The station closed in June 1965 and today the site is now hidden beneath the elevated section of the M6 motorway and surrounding industrial and retail sites.

No. 48185 at Bromford Bridge in March 1953, with a train of loaded wooden-bodied mineral wagons, probably from Toton where the Stanier '8F' was based. The derelict industrial yard behind the signal box was developed with factory units by the late 1960s. Note the ancient Midland Railway or early LM&SR built brake van standing in the platform road, at the rear of yet another freight on the Up goods line.

Evidence of the changes which had taken place within just a few years, with large scale industrial activity now replacing the previously hotch-potch yard, whilst steel-bodied open wagons proliferate throughout the train. 'Crab' 2-6-0 No. 42839 heads west towards Washwood Heath sidings, watched by a handful of spotters on the Up platform. The picture was taken between 1959 and November 1961 while the engine was allocated to Burton. The signal box controlled the approach to Washwood Heath but closed in 1969 when Saltley Power Box was commissioned.

'Crab' 2-6-0 No. 42710 from Burton shed heads east through Bromford Bridge station in 1958, with a Class 'E' express freight which has four fitted 'Shoc Opens' at the head. It had been a Newton Heath engine since it was built at Horwich, as No. 13010 in 1927. The picture dates between October 1961 when AWS was fitted and its transfer to Gorton in July 1963. The works visible in the right background was part of the large Bromford Tube Company site, which had its own sidings alongside the main line.

BR Standard Class '4MT' 4-6-0 No. 75040 in late 1962 or early 1963 at Bromford Bridge, on an eastbound Class 'D' express freight. It was allocated to Derby from September 1962 and has the 17A shedcode which lasted until August 1963, when it became 16C.

Holbeck 'Jubilee' No. 45739 *Ulster* runs through a deserted Bromford Bridge in 1963. This was not surprising since the station was only used when a meeting was held at the nearby Birmingham Race Course and therefore had only the most basic facilities. It closed after the final meeting in June 1965 and the racecourse was replaced by a housing estate.

Lime-stained Saltley '9F' 2-10-0 No. 92057 heads a Class 'J' train of concrete pipes, which is likely to have originated at Stanton. The pipes are carried in ex-LM&SR 3-plank dropside wagons and are heading towards Washwood Heath in late 1963. Bromford Bridge signal box is just visible on the right hand platform and Fort Dunlop with its tower and flagpole is in the centre background.

The well-known Fort Dunlop works were built on a 40 acre site in 1916, with sidings connecting with the Midland Railway line to Water Orton. Traffic consisted of inbound raw materials and coal for the power house, as well as the despatch of finished products. Strangely, an engine shed was never provided, locomotives latterly standing under the loading canopy when not in use. This W. Bagnall 0-4-0ST, Works No. 2648 of 1941 and new to ROF Rotherwas near Hereford, is seen here running as *Dunlop No. 6*. It arrived here from Fred Watkins boiler works at Sling, near Coleford, Gloucestershire in August 1965, having been rebuilt there using the boiler from sister engine WB Works No. 2653. Taken out of use when steam working ceased in 1971, it is now preserved at Shackerstone, Leicestershire. Rail traffic continued at the Fort until around 1988.

Stanier Class '5' No. 44858 at Bromford Bridge in around 1964, on the Down Fast with a Class 'C' express freight, looking towards Castle Bromwich.

Over a hundred '4F' 0-6-0s were still in service as late as 1965, when No. 44057 was photographed running tender first through Bromford Bridge. It has a yellow stripe on the cabside indicating that it was not permitted to work under the overhead wires south of Crewe. The coal-railed tender has a chalked target number '12' and Class 'K' headlamps, indicating it is on a local pick-up working, probably to Water Orton sidings. No. 44057 had been transferred to Bescot from Gorton in December 1964 and moved to Saltley in July before withdrawal in November.

Stanier '8F' No. 48336 on a train of loaded 'Dogfish' ballast hoppers in 1964, crossing the bridge over the River Tame which was immediately before the start of Washwood Heath Up sidings. This was one of seventy-five of the class built at Horwich, entering service in February 1945. It came to the Midlands from Willesden in late 1965, firstly to Bescot and then moving to Saltley from March 1966 until March 1967. It has the mid-1963 modification where the upper lamp bracket was moved down onto the smokebox door, away from live overhead wires, and also large 10ins cab numbers.

Watched by two spotters sitting at the top of the steps, with their bicycles propped up against the railings, two Brush Type '2's, No's D5687 and D5830, stand at Bromford Bridge probably waiting to take a Class '6' train back to their home at Sheffield Tinsley during 1963.

Brand new Brush Type '4's No's D1733 and D1740 running light towards Birmingham at Bromford Bridge. No. D1733 is in the XP64 prototype British Rail blue livery, with the new double arrow symbol on a red background. It made extensive tours around the system with the XP64 prototype blue and grey liveried coaches. Note that even the Brush maker's plate has been repositioned to suit the livery. Both diesels were built at Loughborough and officially entered traffic on the same date in June 1964. After the final loaded acceptance trials run from Derby, the new locomotives did not return to Loughborough. Delivery to their allocated depots was always from Derby shed and this picture appears to have been taken on the delivery run to their new homes on the Western Region.

Another pair of Type '2's, this time of the Derby Sulzer variety, No's D5193 and D5194 plus a brake tender, wait at Bromford Bridge. Train number 8G23 was the 2.52pm Toton to Washwood Heath (No. 2 Back Fan) – so it is likely that the locomotives have come off 8G23, crossed to the Up Goods line, run to Bromford and are about to set back into the Up Sidings for a return working, probably the 7D38 7pm Up Sidings to Toton. Note the two neat square holes in the front doors for possible fitting of additional pipes.

One of the later BR Sulzer Type '2's, No. D7624, in the rain at Bromford Bridge. Train number 4M92 was the 23.45 Carlisle to Washwood Heath from 1964. The first four vehicles of the train are 'Bocars'– bogie carriages stripped of their bodies and used for moving car components. They are sheeted over with BR tarpaulins and are possibly carrying car bodies from Linwood to Coventry for the Rootes car company. No. D7624 was the first of thirty-five Class '25s' to be built by Beyer, Peacock and entered service in July 1965 at Sheffield Tinsley. Bromford Bridge station had been closed by this date, as the long line of headless Midland Railway lamp posts shows.

Washwood Heath and Saltley

Washwood Heath Sidings were situated between Bromford Bridge and Saltley stations. The location offered a considerable number of advantages to the Midland Railway, which required a facility on its line from Derby near to the centre of Birmingham, that was also close to L&NWR and GWR routes to facilitate the easy exchange of traffic. The first part of the sidings was opened in October 1877, initially only on the Down Derby to Birmingham line because the traffic was predominantly inward bound to the city. These

were extended in 1891 and sidings were built on the Up side of the line in January 1918; both were enlarged in the 1930s and featured a small 'Hump Shunting' facility. As a marshalling yard and not a goods yard, Washwood Heath was used to receive and break down incoming trains, marshalling the wagons for onward transmission to other destinations, both local and to other sorting yards all over the country.

No. 92029 is seen departing Washwood Heath Down Sidings towards Saltley station and passing under the former L&NWR Aston to Stechford line. The locomotive was converted from Crosti boiler to standard in August 1960. Its front footplate looks somewhat bent!

BR Standard Class '5MT No. 73004 is dwarfed by the Saltley Gas Works gas holders. No. 73004 has a BR 1 tender with inset coal space. The 10ins cab numbers, rather than the standard 8ins size which it had when new, arose from a Heavy General repair at Cowlairs Works in September/October 1961.

Turning through nearly ninety degrees from the Crosti '9F' photograph above, the view across the main line with the Aston to Stechford line in the background is revealed. Such was the intensity of the traffic that more than one shunting pilot was required in both the Up and Down yards, and No's 13167 and 13248 are captured resting between duties. The pair of 350hp shunters were both products of Derby Works, being released to traffic in August 1955 and May 1956 respectively. No. 13167 was sent new to Saltley but No. 13248 wandered around the Midland Division before finding a home at Saltley in October 1957. They were re-numbered No's D3167 and D3248 in the early 1960s, followed by TOPS No's 08102 and 08180 in April 1974. Withdrawal came in 1981 for No. 08180 but No. 08102 survived to 1988 and luckily was preserved and is currently at the Lincolnshire Wolds Railway.

BRCW Type '3' diesels No's D6526 and D6558 arriving at Bromford Bridge with a loaded oil train, almost certainly the 4M40 04.45am MX Fawley to Bromford Bridge, due at 10.45. This was one of the heaviest trains to be seen in the Birmingham area at this time, normally consisting of fifty-four 45-ton tanks plus a Southern Railway 'Queen Mary' bogie brake van. This picture, probably taken in 1965, is looking north west from Bromford Lane bridge at the east end of the Washwood Heath Yards.

Saltley

The Fowler 2-6-4Ts were a mainstay of Saltley shed's passenger service for many years. All of those pictured here were in the final batch which were fitted with the so-called 'limousine' cabs. These had side windows and full height doors instead of the large cut-outs either side of the gangway; these had proved unacceptable when operating bunker-first as the incoming air blew coal around the cab making conditions extremely bad for the crew.

No. 42416, pictured on an empty stock working passing through Saltley station, arrived from Bangor in August 1960 and stayed until transferred to Stafford in May 1964. The fact that it returned within a month and was withdrawn a week later suggests that this may have been a 'paper' transfer. The train has originated from Saltley Carriage sidings and is probably en route to New Street station. The building on the right is the former Midland Railway Carriage & Wagon Company works, which became part of the Metropolitan-Cammell group in 1929.

No. 42421 was at Saltley for longer than No. 42416, from August 1960 until it too was transferred to Stafford, in June 1964, and was withdrawn there two months later. It is seen here in 1962 passing Saltley Sidings signal box on a transfer freight working, with Brothertons Chemical works to the left. The cooling towers and chimneys of Nechells Power Station are visible in the right background.

Fowler 2-6-4T No. 42400 on a Class 'K' trip freight working on the Down Lawley Street Goods lines approaching Saltley Station. The train, which is made up almost entirely of covered vans, will have originated from either Water Orton or Washwood Heath sidings and is bound for Lawley Street. No. 42400 arrived at Saltley at the same time as No. 42416, in August 1960 and was also transferred to Stafford in June 1964.

No. 45653 *Barham* at Saltley on a duty far removed from that when first introduced by the LM&SR. It has a 2F Saltley shedplate and was on loan there from Blackpool between March 1963 and April 1964. No. 45653 has a part-welded tender, one of only seven 'Jubilees' to be paired with this type – this was probably because these were all built with Class '5's and it was expensive to fully repaint them from black to green livery. The pale blue container at the front of the train had recently been used to convey Fyffes bananas. The gas works are clearly visible behind the 'Jubilee'.

A Western Region 'Modified Hall' from Tyseley, No. 6971 *Athelhampton Hall*, passing through Saltley towards Camp Hill on the Down Goods line in 1962. It was very strange to see coal empties going this way, so we suggest they were actually loaded, perhaps with power station slack and the train is possibly the 7V22 6.10pm Washwood Heath to Banbury. No. 6971 lasted until late 1964. In the background is the Saltley Sidings signal box and in the distance the skyline is dominated by the power station and gas holders. At one time all the exchange freight trains between Washwood Heath and Bordesley were worked by ex-LM&SR locomotives. In the early 1950s, 'Crabs', Class '8's and Class '5's were the usual classes used.

'Modified Hall' No. 7929 *Wyke Hall*, also on the Down Goods at Saltley station but on 6th April 1963; the locomotive appears to be pulling hard, supporting the theory that these trains were carrying coal slack. According to the 1959 Working Time Table, 'Halls' were allowed as far as Water Orton to collect and deliver inter-regional freights but were only permitted to use the reception and departure roads. At Washwood Heath Up and Down sidings, there were similar restrictions with access allowed to certain roads. The only other GWR tender type allowed were the Class '2251' 0-6-0s, which had the same access as a Midland '3F' 0-6-0.

Saltley shed

The former Midland Railway shed at Saltley dates back to 1854, when the first building was erected on the site of what later became Lawley Street. It was moved to the opposite side of the running lines in 1868 and became No. 1 shed. No. 2 shed was opened in 1876 and No. 3 in 1900, becoming the railway's second busiest shed after Derby. The depot was equipped with a mechanical ash disposal and coaling plant by the LM&SR in the 1930s. Most of its allocation over the years consisted of freight classes and tank engines used on local shunting and suburban duties. It was coded 21A from 1935 until September 1963, then becoming 2E, and was closed as a steam shed in March 1967. A three-track diesel refuelling and maintenance depot was built in the shed yard and remained in use until 2005.

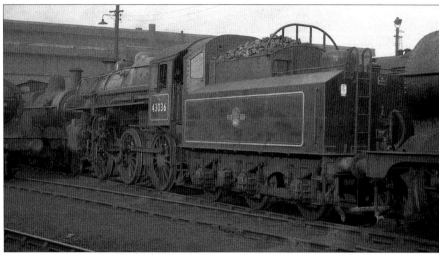

One of several Ivatt '4MT' 2-6-0s shedded at Saltley, No. 43036 shows clearly the safety bar fitted to the tenders on some of the class. Seen here on 19th March 1961, it had been transferred to Saltley from Bristol in 1953 and was there for almost ten years, apart from a two month loan spell at Neasden in 1960, finally moving away to Trafford Park in September 1962.

'Crab' 2-6-0 No. 42827 poses in front of the mechanical coaling tower on 18th February 1962. On the left is the ash disposal plant, with two open wagons already filled. The electrically operated coaling tower was built of reinforced concrete and had two 150 ton bunkers. Coal was raised by wagon on the outside of the tower, under the control of an attendant in the cabin located at the base of the plant. The ash plant was steel framed, with a winch room clad with metal corrugated sheeting. Locomotives being emptied would stand on either side of the structure, the centre road being where the wagons removing the ash were placed. The ash would be emptied into hoppers that were then hoisted on rails until positioned above the wagon for discharging.

No. 42827 was a long-standing resident at Saltley, based there from April 1947 until June 1964. This rear view taken on the same date as the picture above shows that it had one of the later snap-head riveted Fowler 3,500 gallon tenders, which were built with additional coal rails. Note the pile of fire-irons on the Midland Railway stand to the right of the tender – that's where they all went!

'Royal Scot' No. 46103 *Royal Scots Fusilier* stands adjacent to a Stanier '8F' in one of the roundhouses on 18th February 1962. It was one of eleven rebuilt Class '7Ps' – nine 'Scots' and two 'Patriots' – transferred to Saltley in mid-1961. They were probably brought in to work excursion trains in place of the '9F' 2-10-0s used in the previous year, although *The Railway Observer* reported that they were used on freight duties from Washwood Heath, including the ignominy of Bordesley Junction trip workings. All left within a year, mostly to Carlisle Upperby and seven of these went almost straight into store. No. 46103 spent twelve months at Saltley, from June 1961 to June 1962, after which it moved briefly to Carlisle Upperby and Leeds Holbeck, before it was withdrawn at the end of the year. No. 46103 was the first of the class to be rebuilt with a tapered boiler, emerging from Crewe Works in June 1943.

Double chimneyed '9F' 2-10-0 No. 92205 in the light from the coaling stage at Saltley, probably in 1963 when it was allocated to the Southern Region at Eastleigh. It has a strange looking arrangement of lamp irons, with one halfway down at each side of the smokebox. This was done on five '9Fs' when they were transferred from the Western Region to accommodate SR route discs. No. 92205 also had a standard BR bracket attached to the smokebox handrail, a legacy from 1960 when it worked over the Somerset & Dorset line, and used to fix the reporting number board. It has no upper lamp bracket, this having been removed for safety reasons by November 1963, because it had been moved a few years earlier to the smokebox rim from the top of the smokebox door.

Saltley No. 3 roundhouse seems positively light and airy in this 1965 picture. It had been rebuilt in 1956 with a new roof, higher walls and a long glazed panel. However, all was not well as the roof was removed in the early 1960s and demolition followed soon after the closure to steam. The three engines in the centre are '9F' 2-10-0 No. 92215 from nearby Tyseley, Stanier Class '5' No. 45255 from Newton Heath and one of Saltley's own '8F' 2-8-0s, No. 48339.

The eastern approaches to New Street station were complex, reflecting the development over the years of the L&NWR and the Midland Railway in Birmingham. It is easiest to take the Midland line first and to describe the junctions it encountered en route to New Street. Passing Saltley shed, the first junction was Landor Street, where the Birmingham avoiding lines, originally known as the Aston Curve and used primarily for freight, branched off. This was also known as the Camp Hill line and the gradients and low line speed required bankers from Duddeston Road just outside Saltley. They went as far as Bordesley for GWR exchange traffic, Camp Hill or Kings Heath, depending upon the load and the train engine driver's requirements; this practice continued right up until the 1980s.

The line then curved sharply passing under the L&NWR Coventry via Stechford line, which it joined at Grand Junction. This was closely followed by the L&NWR Aston line joining at Proof House Junction, where there was a flyover.

Turning now back to the Camp Hill lines from Landor Street, the first junction was St. Andrews, where lines heading into New Street (via Grand Junction) were encountered. Next was Bordesley Junction, where lines joined the GWR line just south of Moor Street at Bordesley South Junction. Back on the Camp Hill line, the route was high on an embankment as it climbed over the GWR lines to the summit. It continued through the Birmingham southern suburbs, before joining the Midland Railway New Street to Bromsgrove/Evesham line at the triangle of Lifford, just north of Kings Norton.

Landor Street Junction

The last four Great Western railcars were operated as twin-coupled railcar units, the forerunner of today's diesel multiple units. With the driving compartments only at the outer ends of the set, buffet and toilet facilities could be provided for 104 seated passengers and if a standard corridor coach was added between the two cars, another 70 seats could be added, allowing them to be used on longer-distance workings such as Birmingham to Cardiff. The units, which were built in 1941-2, were identical in technical details to the earlier single car, No's 19-33, series. This set, pictured at Landor Street around 1955, is probably on a special working, possibly to Derby. They were often used at this time on enthusiast specials, such as one organised by the Birmingham Locomotive Club to Buxton and a Talyllyn Railway Preservation Society AGM working. The water tower on the left supplied the water columns at Lawley Street Goods Station.

A second picture, taken after the railcar had moved further away, shows that the train is on the Up Camp Hill line at Landor Street Junction. The signal is off for the Up main line, the other signal is for the Up goods line. The engines to the far right are on Saltley shed, whilst in the distance is the gas works and to the left, Lawley Street. Adjacent to the signal box is a water column frequently used by passing trains and also the cabin where Saltley men – driver, fireman and guard – waited to relieve crews arriving at Landor Street. The train crews were booked to complete the walk in ten minutes from Saltley shed to the relief cabin. The line to the left of the signal is the Midland Railway curve to Proof House and New Street.

Class '4F' 0-6-0 No. 43940 in 1964, on the Up Camp Hill line approaching Landor Street Junction. The overbridge is for the L&NWR main line to Stechford and just beyond the bridge is Brickyard Crossing, with its signal box. No. 43940 is quite possibly working 'Target 49', the 12.05 pm Selly Oak-Water Orton, which was booked for a Saltley '4F' and conveyed Cadbury's traffic, although there is a chalked number '18' on the bufferbeam. The front end of the '4F' has received the attention of one of the more artistic shed staff who has painted on the 2E shedcode and, to make certain, SALTLEY on the bufferbeam. No. 43940 was built for the Midland Railway in 1921 by Armstrong Whitworth and lasted until October 1964. Note the shunter's pole on the engine in front of the smokebox.

The 'Peaks' were the mainstay of the North East-South West services through Birmingham, from the early 1960s right through the 1970s. No. D21 leans into the curve at Landor Street Junction, heading for New Street in 1965 with the 08.10 Sheffield to Paignton and Penzance (SX) or Penzance (SO). The 55A shedplate on the yellow warning panel shows that it was based at Leeds Holbeck.

St. Andrews Junction

Class '9F' 2-10-0 No. 92237, viewed from the signal box at St. Andrews Junction, with a train of twenty empty Esso tankers probably en route for the Fawley oil terminal at Southampton; the four barrier vehicles are all vans and include a GWR fruit van. The 45-ton GLW tanks did not enter service until 1965 and are pretty dirty, whilst the Ebbw Junction allocated '9F' was withdrawn in September of that year, so it must be close to that date. Southern Region BRC&W Type '3' diesels began working on the Fawley-Bromford Bridge trains in March 1963 and by June it was reported that all were diesel hauled; the locomotives were stabled overnight at Saltley, so this would have been a rare steam substitution. The other possibility is that this is the 4V55 18.10 Coleshill WMGB-Milford Haven empty naptha tanks, which would perhaps be more in keeping with the short length of the train.

Ex-GWR Class '57xx' 'Pannier' tank No. 9774 takes the right hand route at St. Andrews Junction in 1965, possibly with a Bordesley to Washwood Heath control special of coal empties. It had been transferred from Wellington in August 1964 to Tyseley, from where it was withdrawn in late 1966. The brake lever tells us that the first wagon was an L&NER built hopper.

An unidentified Class '9F' 2-10-0 at St. Andrews Junction in 1965, with a train of covered 'Bocar' bogie wagons transporting car parts, which suggests this train is possibly a Longbridge tripper.

Grimy Brush Type '4' No. D1708 at St. Andrews Junction with a freight bound for the Southern Region, the 12.20 Washwood Heath-Eastleigh via Bordesley Junction, in 1965.

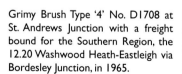

4 – Birmingham New Street

New Street station was opened by the London & North Western Railway in June 1854, replacing the original London & Birmingham Railway terminus at Curzon Street and the Grand Junction terminus at Lawley Street, which both became goods depots. It took seven years to build and involved a large amount of demolition work, with approaches through tunnels at both ends of the station. The Midland Railway were tenants, with extensive running rights for their trains between Derby and Bristol. As traffic increased, the facilities became increasingly congested and, in 1883, work began on the 'Midland Extension', built to the south of Queen Street, which then effectively divided the enlarged station into two sides. The Midland platforms were covered by an overall twin-arched roof, designed to harmonise with the massive 840 feet by 212 feet single span arch of the L&NWR roof, which at the time of its construction was the largest single span roof in the world. From then onwards, New Street was essentially operated as two semi-independent stations, even into the early days of British Railways. The North Western side had two Up and two Down main lines, five bay platforms and three main platforms, whilst the 'Midland' also had two Up and two Down main lines, and three main platforms but only one bay platform.

The orientation of the station is east to west, trains from the London and Derby direction approaching from the east through the 286 yard long North and South Tunnels respectively, and then under Worcester Street bridge. Services to the north west and south west passed under Hill Street and Navigation Street bridges, before plunging into the 760 yard Monument Lane and the 176 yard Suffolk Street tunnels respectively. However, to the confusion of many an observer, the layout of lines in the Birmingham area allowed northbound or southbound trains to leave New Street in either direction, which proved very useful when the electrification and rebuilding work started in the 1960s.

Until replaced by the horrendous (now listed!) corrugated concrete power box in 1964, New Street was controlled by six signal boxes. At the east end, No. 1 dealt with the L&NWR side and No. 2 with the Midland side. No. 3, which was perched up in the roof in the centre of the station, shared the duties of No. 1. At the west end, No. 4 was responsible for the Midland platforms, with No. 5, the biggest of the boxes, looking after the L&NWR lines and No. 6, a small building at track level partly concealed by Navigation Street bridge, controlling movements at the end of Platform 1 and the Stour Valley bays.

Despite several plans to improve it during the first half of the 20th century, New Street changed little, until the effects of bomb damage between 1940 and 1942, on the North Western side overall roof, compounded years of neglect and rendered it beyond economic repair, and so it was dismantled. The work took over two years to complete and it was replaced by individual utilitarian steel canopies over each platform, although there was one much needed improvement when electric lighting was installed at the same time. Track circuiting and colour light signals were installed on the L&NWR approach lines, allowing No. 3 signal box to be eliminated; the mechanical signalling on the Midland side was left unchanged. Also, from 7th October 1946, new platform numbers were introduced to replace the confusing system which had been in use since the opening of the Midland Extension in 1885, where each platform had one number irrespective of the number of faces.

The 1950s saw only cosmetic changes with a full and long overdue repaint in 1952, new signage and train indicators, and updated refreshment facilities. However, all was about to change with the electrification of the London Midland line between Stafford and Rugby, via Wolverhampton, Birmingham and Coventry. The old station was totally demolished and replaced by a much criticised, although operationally much improved station, built beneath a massive concrete apron that supported a major new shopping centre above.

Steam's final bow at New Street was unplanned. On Thursday 17th November 1966, a Coventry-New Street DMU failed between Stechford and Adderley Park. Ivatt '4MT' 2-6-0 No. 43002 was in the yard at Stechford and was summoned to propel the unit to New Street. The rebuilding of the station was already largely complete and No. 43002's smoke was decidedly unwelcome on the new shiny white tiles. This was just two days after the first electric locomotive had entered the station to test the overhead. The first electric train, 'AM4' (Class '304') set No. 029, entered the station on a test run demonstrated to the press only eight days later, ahead of a limited electric service from 5th December. From 2nd January 1967, local services to Coventry, Wolverhampton and Walsall were taken over by 'AM4' and new 'AM10' (Class '310') EMUs.

Fortunately, this station too has had its day and a £550 million redevelopment began in late 2009 to create a station worthy of the city and to reflect its status as the busiest interchange in the United Kingdom. The official website providing details of the project described it as '*dark, unwelcoming and overcrowded with poor access for passengers*'. Over 140,000 passengers now use the station every day, more than double the number it was designed to handle when rebuilt in the 1960s.

Those unused platform barrows were always handy for trainspotters. These two, with their well-stocked bags, look as though they were there for the day. Behind them, a Stanier Class '5' raises the roof and there is one of the small 204bhp diesel shunters, No. D2395, which became Class '03' under TOPS, that were used as station pilots in the mid-1960s. This one came to Monument Lane in March 1962 from Bushbury and worked from there until January 1967.

The 1950s

Rebuilt 'Patriot' No. 45527 *Southport* at Birmingham New Street in early 1950, waiting to depart with a London train. It had possibly just arrived from Liverpool – where it was allocated to Edge Hill – and had been rebuilt in September 1948.

Crewe North '2P' 4-4-0 No. 40527 waits at Platform 5 with a Down service made up of ex-L&NWR stock in 1952. It had been transferred from Northampton in early 1951 and stayed at 5A for slightly over two years, moving to Chester Northgate in May 1953.

The fireman is up on the tender bringing the coal forward before the departure of rebuilt 'Scot' No. 46141 The North Staffordshire Regiment in April 1952. It appears to have both a later 7P and its earlier 6P power classifications above the cab number.

Former L&NWR 'Coal Tank' No. 58900 in 1953. Based at nearby Monument Lane shed, it had been a New Street pilot for the previous two years but was transferred to Swansea Paxton Street in March 1954 and replaced by No. 58903 from Bangor, which was the last of its class to work as a New Street pilot engine.

Looking east in October 1953 under Queens Drive bridge and towards Worcester Street Tunnel, as Stanier 'Jubilee' No. 45680 *Camperdown* waits for an incoming train in the short siding immediately in front of No. 2 signal box. This box, which had originally been built by the L&NWR, controlled the Midland side at this end of New Street station. Camperdown was shedded at Manchester Longsight from October 1947 until October 1960, when it was transferred to Edge Hill. The starting signal is a filthy L&NWR bracket fitted with supplementary shunting signals below each of the full size arms. Note the signal ladder fitted in front of the main post and curving at the top – this was standard L&NWR practice.

Looking west down Platform 10 on the Midland side in 1954, with a Stanier Class '5' on the through road to the right and another in the bay Platform 11 to the left. The overall twin-arched roof with spans of around 60 feet each was built in the late 19th century when the 'Midland Extension' was added to the original L&NWR station.

The Ivatt '4MT' 2-6-0s were a common sight on the Midland Division side of Birmingham New Street on station pilot duties, and they also worked local passenger services and empty stock trains. The engines were regulars on the Redditch to Ashchurch branch, working the passenger services right up to closure in June 1963. Saltley's No. 43017 is at the west end of Platform 10, under the high roof on the Midland side of the station in the mid-1950s. No. 43017 had been transferred to Bath from Saltley in December 1949 but moved back there by the end of 1953 and stayed until 1964, when it left for Bletchley. This picture was taken after the replacement of its original double chimney in February 1954.

Both classes of Ivatt 2-6-0 worked as New Street pilots in the 1950s, as shown by this picture of '2MT' No. 46425. When built in November 1948, it went straight to Bescot shed where it remained until withdrawn in September 1965, apart from a month in North Wales on loan to Rhyl in summer 1953. The early LM&SR coach with Stones ventilators looks positively modern in its stylish crimson and cream livery.

Fairburn 2-6-4T No. 42267 of Monument Lane, taken after its March 1958 Heavy General repair at Crewe and before February 1962 when it moved to Stafford. It had been resident at the L&NWR shed since February 1948.

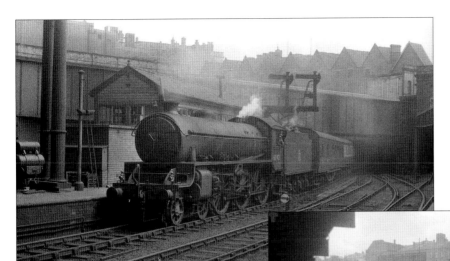

No. 61142, a Thompson 'B1' from Immingham shed, passes No. 2 signal box as it arrives at Platform 9 from Cleethorpes. This was a regular daily working which brought the ex-L&NER class to Birmingham. They would go to Saltley shed for coal and water before returning to the Eastern Region. Withdrawn from Nottingham's Colwick shed in September 1963, No. 61142 would return to the West Midlands for its final journey, when it went to Cashmore's of Great Bridge for scrapping in December of that year.

The crowds of expectant passengers are surprisingly small as they wait on Platform 3 for Class '5' No. 44914 to bring in their train for the 'City of Birmingham Holiday Express' in 1956. These excursion trains provided a cheap holiday for the local workers and the cost was £5 for five different day's outings in a week. Typical destinations included the North Wales Coast (Rhyl, Colwyn Bay, or Llandudno), London, Matlock or Buxton, Brighton and Southport.

The immaculate paintwork of 'Britannia' 4-6-2 No. 70037 *Hereward The Wake* suggests that this picture was taken in 1956, after the completion of a Heavy General repair at Crewe; it may have been working its way back home to the Eastern Region. The 'Pacific' was allocated to Stratford depot in London from new in December 1952 until 1959. As with many of its class, it moved to the London Midland Region to see out its final years at Carlisle.

Stanier '2MT' 2-6-2T No. 40108, one of the New Street station pilots which succeeded the L&NWR 'Coal Tanks', shunts a GWR diagram DC4 'Cordon' gas tank wagon into the parcels bay. The class was by some distance the least successful of Stanier's designs for the London Midland & Scottish Railway. No. 40108 was allocated to Monument Lane shed from June 1954 until late 1960.

Ivatt '2MT' 2-6-2T No. 41223, seen alongside No. 1 signal box at the east end of New Street, was at Monument Lane from April 1955 until March 1956, when it was transferred to Ryecroft shed at Walsall. No. 41223 was working one of the steam push-pull services introduced on 30th September 1954. These two-coach trains initially ran only to Sutton Coldfield but were extended to the next station, Four Oaks, within a few weeks. They were replaced by the new diesel multiple unit service which ran through to Lichfield City from 5th March 1956. The Thompson full brake has been added onto the rear of the push-pull service.

This new Derby 'Lightweight' DMU, waiting to depart from Platform 4 to Four Oaks, a suburb just north of Sutton Coldfield, is attracting lots of attention from the platform. Prior to 5th March 1956, when regular interval New Street-Four Oaks-Lichfield City diesel services started, an inaugural return trip was made on 28th February by a party composed of representatives of the civic and business communities of Birmingham, Sutton Coldfield, and Lichfield, and it is likely that this picture was taken on that day.

Parallel boiler 'Patriot' No. 45511 *Isle of Man* departs from the west end of Platform 6 on a Manchester express. The picture was taken in the mid-1950s, when it was allocated to Camden.

Bushbury 'Jubilee' No. 45741 *Leinster* at Platform 6, waiting to depart with a London to Wolverhampton express in the late 1950s. It was at Wolverhampton shed throughout the 1950s, apart from a six month spell at Edge Hill in 1951, moving away to Carlisle Upperby when the London Midland through services to London were withdrawn in November 1959. The canopies on this side of the station were replaced after the Second World War using surplus ARP steel covered by asbestos sheets and were supposed to be temporary structures until a new overall roof was constructed.

Built as No. M4749 in February 1948, this was the second Stanier Class '5' fitted with the Caprotti valve gear which caused such a radical change in appearance, compared to the standard Walschaerts valve gear engines. The running plate had to be set over a foot lower to clear the camboxes and reversing gearboxes, resulting in the cut-off cab sides, whilst the outside steam pipes, cranked to clear the drive-gear on the top of the cannon boxes at the top of the cylinders, were very prominent. No. 44749 was allocated to Longsight shed from new until September 1960, when it was transferred to Speke Junction; this picture was taken before it was fitted with AWS in September 1959. As was often the case, the tank filler on its part-welded tender has been left open. The first vehicle behind the tender is an ex-L&NWR 6-wheeled combination truck, probably in use moving spares between works and running sheds.

'Jubilee' No. 45734 *Meteor* is blowing off at the safety valves as it waits to depart from Platform 3 with 'The Midlander' to Coventry and London Euston in 1958. The Up train used the Stour Valley route from Wolverhampton to Birmingham, instead of the Grand Junction route taken by the Down train, and reached Euston in 2 hours 10 minutes from New Street. No. 45734 had been shedded at Bushbury since July 1951, having had two previous spells there, and with its shedmates was a regular performer on the Euston expresses. A BRC&W Co. DMU waiting to work a Coventry service is just visible on the left of the picture and the rear of the Queen's Hotel provides an impressive backdrop. It must have been quite hard to sleep in the rooms on this side!

Crewe North 'Royal Scot' No. 46159 *The Royal Air Force* on a southbound express in 1958, is watched by a group of spotters crowded onto one of those handy parcels trolleys at the end of Platform 3. The flat-roofed canopies mounted on bare steel frames, which replaced the original single span arched roof on the ex-L&NWR side of the station which had been severely damaged in the Second World War, gave little weather protection.

Prototype diesels

In this lovely period shot, No. 10800 is back on home ground on 12th March 1955 after unsuccessful trials and testing on the Southern and Eastern regions in the previous three years. During this time, it had been laid-up in Brighton Works from June 1953 until February 1954, and again between April and December 1954. Its headcode discs are for an Empty Coaching Stock train, so presumably it will take the coaches away from Platform 5 to Monument Lane. No. 10800 was to spend nine months of 1956 in Derby Works and, not surprisingly, was withdrawn in 1959 after managing to run less than 25,000 miles in the previous two years.

Birmingham New Street frequently saw the early main line diesels after they were all transferred to the London Midland Region in the winter of 1954-5, including the North British 827bhp Bo-Bo No. 10800, which is watched by a large throng of spotters as it arrives from Peterborough, probably in summer 1955. On weekdays, the diesel, which was based at Rugby shed at the time, worked the 10.25am from Peterborough (ex-Yarmouth) to Birmingham. It then went onto Monument Lane shed, coming off in the afternoon to work the 3.55pm from New Street to Yarmouth back to Peterborough.

A copy of an official notice which was somewhat disregarded! It is interesting that it only applied to boys, of unspecified age, and not to men.

> BRITISH RAILWAYS
> **"ENGINE SPOTTING"**
> AT
> BIRMINGHAM
> NEW STREET
> STATION
>
> British Railways announce with regret that, in the interests of safety, the practice of boys remaining on the platforms and railways premises at **BIRMINGHAM NEW STREET STATION** for the purpose of engine-spotting and watching trains
>
> **IS PROHIBITED**

The second of the London Midland & Scottish Railway designed Co-Cos, No. 10001, arrives at New Street from London in 1958. The two diesels had both run their highest annual mileages in the previous year, working singly on trains to Manchester and Wolverhampton and in multiple to Scotland. Their performance declined slightly in 1958 with No. 10001 catching fire and, thereafter, they were very much neglected as the new British Railways' designs came into service, although No. 10001 remained in traffic until March 1966.

The 1960s

'Coronation' 'Pacific's were very rarely seen at New Street until their last few years in service, after the diesels displaced them from their duties on the West Coast main line. No. 46239 *City of Chester* gets underway from Platform 3 with a London bound train. The picture was probably taken in 1963, as the Type '4' diesel has received a yellow warning panel and these were not introduced until mid-1962; No. 46239 was fitted with AWS in March 1959 but was one of those 'Coronations' that stayed in green livery after the 1957-8 change to crimson lake for about half of the class. The steps of New Street No. 1 signal box are in the foreground.

The Railway Observer reported that, in July 1963, six 'Coronation' 'Pacific's had been working on the Euston-Wolverhampton trains in place of the usual English Electric Type '4' diesels, No's 46236/40/45/54/56/57. No. 46240 *City of Coventry* passes under Hill Street Bridge as it departs on a Euston-Wolverhampton express. The steps of No. 5 signal box are just visible on the right of the picture.

Diesel interlude

English Electric Type '4's were rostered for all the Euston trains from May 1961 up to electrification in 1966. Camden allocated No. D377 entered traffic in June 1962 and is shown here in August, probably never having been cleaned! In the right background the tall crane is working on the construction of the famous 'Rotunda' building, which was completed in early 1965. In the centre is the rear of the Odeon cinema and theatre in New Street, which is the only one of seven similar built in the late 1930s still in use as a cinema today.

English Electric Type '4' No. D300 enters Platform 9 past No. 2 signal box with the 'Pines Express' from Manchester to Bournemouth West via the Somerset & Dorset line. It is arriving from the eastern direction and will have travelled via Witton and Aston so that it is facing west on departure. It was photographed on 31st August 1962, just over a week before the start of the Winter Time Table, in which the train was diverted via Snow Hill and Reading West. (Robert Darlaston)

BR Sulzer Type '2' No. D5013 at the western end of the station under Hill Street Bridge on 30th July 1962. It is probably taking the stock out to the carriage sidings at Monument Lane after working a train from Peterborough. The building on the right has a large neon sign proclaiming that it is 'Guinness Time' and 'Guinness is Good for You'.

The same BR Sulzer Type '2', No. D5013, pictured a week later, on 7th August 1962, about to depart with a Peterborough train. Note the 'GE' prefix to the Mark 1 coach number.

Demolition

The British Railways publicity machine described the redevelopment of New Street thus: '*To accommodate the increased and accelerated traffic New Street station is being completely rebuilt on lines which will conform to civic modernization as well as communications. The new main entrance from Smallbrook will give access to twelve through platforms designed for the utmost flexibility of working. Platforms will be connected by escalators to a service deck, surmounting which will be a third tier comprising restaurants, cinema, dance hall and other recreational facilities.*' While the work was carried out, the principal trains to and from London were diverted to Snow Hill, providing the former GWR station with an Indian Summer that lasted until early 1967.

The first blows are struck. Demolition workers begin the task of rebuilding New Street: Platform 11 on 9th April 1964. (Robert Darlaston)

A year later in March 1965 and the rebuilding is well advanced. This picture shows the remains of Queen's Drive, with the former L&NWR platforms on the left, and contrasts with the newly completed twenty-storey, 266 feet high Rotunda tower. This now iconic building was much derided when first built but when there were plans to demolish it in the 1980s, when the Bull Ring area was again redeveloped, these were vigorously opposed by the local populace. In August 2000, it received Grade II listed building status and was converted for residential use, re-opening in 2008. The tall building on the right is part of the Bull Ring Centre. (Robert Darlaston)

A view of the eastern end in March 1965 shows the L&NWR side of the station is still largely untouched. The workmen in the foreground appear to have downed tools for lunch. (Robert Darlaston)

On 28th September 1965, No. 1 signal box still remains in this view from the south end of newly completed Platform 6, with the old (L&NWR) Platform 5 at the left. When the Rotunda was constructed a tower crane was used, which was located to the side of the reinforced concrete central core. Due to its proximity to the railway tunnel below, the main load was built on to a twin ring of piled foundations directly beneath the circular structural core. The tower was originally used for commercial purposes, with a very large office occupied by Lloyds Bank in the structure below. (Robert Darlaston)

This further view taken on the same day but from the new Platform 6 shows the massive concrete apron, which closed in the new station and made it so unattractive, edging towards the tracks. (Robert Darlaston)

On 1st December 1965, in a similar view to that taken in March, Queen's Drive has completely disappeared as large amounts of concrete have been installed above the tracks. English Electric Type '4' No. D335 waits with the 13.40 to Manchester, while work progresses on the old L&NWR platforms to the left. (Robert Darlaston)

The site of the old L&NWR platforms on 3rd March 1966, with the station offices once on Platform 1 and the Queen's Hotel above. (Robert Darlaston)

On the same day, this picture shows work is progress on Platforms 1-3 but 4 and 5 are now in use. It is incredible to think that the station remained open throughout this complete reconstruction. (Robert Darlaston)

After the rebuilding

The concrete has already started to cover the station in this view of 'AL6' No. E3147 after arrival from Euston in 1967, with what we believe is a Fridays Only relief. It was renumbered No. 86211 in August 1973 and was written off after an accident at Colwich in 1986.

Initially, the express passenger work was shared between the new 'AL6s' and the other early electric classes, of which the English Electric built 'AL3's were one of the less successful types. No. E3026 is seen departing south from Birmingham New Street in around 1967. It was stored at Bury from late 1968 until June 1972, when it went to Doncaster Works for refurbishment and became No. 83003 in January 1973. It had a short life after that and was withdrawn in 1975 following a serious accident at Watford.

The sign for the Birmingham Shopping Centre above the ramp to the multi-storey car park is visible above 'AL6' electric No. E3159 on the 10.10 Euston-Wolverhampton on 2nd September 1972. In the five years since it was built, it has acquired full yellow ends and lost the diamond cross-arm pantograph, having been one of only ten originally built with this type. No. E3159 was built in July 1966 by Vulcan Foundry and had no less than four different TOPS identities, No's 86028, 86328, 86428 and 86628.

An early 1970s visit to New Street would see a constant stream of 'Peaks' on the South West to North East cross-country expresses, train reporting number 1M88 being the 06.25 Plymouth-Liverpool service. Blue liveried No. 24, shorn of its 'D' prefix, arrives at New Street on 4th September 1972. Nose-end doors were never fitted to this member of the class but the headcode boxes had been positioned to allow for them. It would become No. 45027 in 1975 and remained in service until May 1981.

5 – *City of Birmingham* through the streets

'Coronation' 'Pacific' No. 46235 *City of Birmingham* was selected for preservation in the National Collection. Although it carried the name *City of Birmingham* from new in 1939, No 6235 was not officially named until March 1945, at a ceremony at New Street station when the city's coat of arms was added above the nameplate. It was the first of the class to be built with a double chimney and the first of those originally built with streamlined casings to be de-streamlined, in April 1946.

No. 46235 was withdrawn from Crewe North in September 1964 and taken into Crewe Works for restoration to its final running condition, in British Railways green livery. After this was completed

in January 1965, *City of Birmingham* was taken to Nuneaton shed for storage while its new resting place at Birmingham's Science & Industry Museum was being readied. No 46235 was moved to Saltley shed immediately prior to its transfer to the new museum in Newhall Street on 20th May 1966. From there, it was taken to Lawley Street goods depot for its final journey through the city's streets by low loader.

After closure of the Science & Industry Museum in 1997, *City of Birmingham* was moved in 2000 into the Thinktank, Birmingham's new science museum, which opened at Millennium Point on Eastside, in September 2001.

Ready to leave Lawley Street on a low loader owned by Robert Wynn and Sons Ltd, a specialist haulage firm based in South Wales.

The tender squeezes under the railway overbridge on what is now Lawley Middleway; hopefully the locomotive will do the same.

Going along the Coventry Road towards the centre. The 'temporary' fly-over to the left was removed nearly twenty years later, in 1983.

The traffic in Digbeth is building up nicely behind No. 46235.

Having reached the top of the slope from Digbeth, the load is passing the now demolished Bull Ring Shopping Centre.

No. 46235 creating quite a stir among the locals in the Bull Ring area.

Almost there – coming down Newhall Street a short distance from the Science Museum.

It is not easy to reverse round a 'Coronation' in the City streets.

Both engine and tender have now safely arrived at the site of the new museum, and the rain looks as if it has just stopped.

Job done and the sun is out – all that is needed now is to build the walls and roof.

6 – London Midland Region in the north Birmingham suburbs

The London Midland Region had two suburban lines in the north Birmingham area, in addition to local trains which ran on its main lines to the north west. One was built by the L&NWR, initially to the prosperous suburban town of Sutton Coldfield and later extended through to Lichfield. The second, which crossed over the L&NWR line at Sutton Coldfield, was formerly owned by the Midland Railway and ran from Castle Bromwich, on its line to Derby, across the north of the city to Walsall and Wolverhampton.

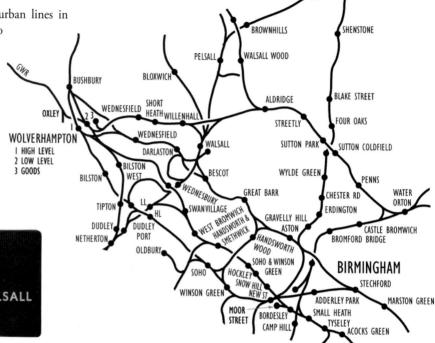

FOR TRAINS TO
LICHFIELD CITY
BIRMINGHAM AND WALSALL

Birmingham New Street to Lichfield

The former L&NWR line from Birmingham New Street to Lichfield, which is now part of the electrified Birmingham 'Cross-City' line, was built in several sections over the years from 1837 until 1884, when it finally reached Lichfield. Initially, most trains ran only to the suburban town of Sutton Coldfield, with all eventually extended the short distance to the next station north, its prosperous satellite of Four Oaks; over time, more ran through to Lichfield. The service was reduced by half during the Second World War and by 1954 had declined still further, with just fourteen trains each day. Things changed considerably when an hourly motor train service was introduced to Sutton Coldfield in May 1955 and this was soon extended to Four Oaks, in July. Three auto-fitted Ivatt '2MT' 2-6-2Ts

were transferred to Monument Lane to work the two-coach trains. In March 1956, they were replaced by new two-car Derby 'Lightweight' diesel multiple units, which provided a half-hourly service to Four Oaks and an hourly service to Lichfield throughout the day. There were now 35 trains each day, which was back up to the pre-war frequency. The impact of the diesels was significant with passenger journeys up from 742,481 in 1955-6 to 2,512,397 in 1957-8, an almost threefold increase within two years. The success of the service resulted in the Derby 'Lightweights' being replaced from the start of the Summer 1958 Time Table by three-car Metropolitan Cammell units, Class '101' under TOPS, which were newly delivered from the manufacturer beginning in April of that year.

Gravelly Hill

Ivatt '2MT' 2-6-2T No. 41320 propels a two-coach push-pull set on a New Street-Four Oaks service in mid-1955 at Gravelly Hill, a place better known nowadays as the location of the 'Spaghetti Junction' motorway interchange. Of the regular '2MT's on the push-pull service at this time, No. 41320 was the most travelled, having been reallocated eleven times before it arrived at Monument Lane from Bangor in April 1955, including two spells at Ryecroft.

Gravelly Hill Station in the late 1960s looking towards Sutton Coldfield and Lichfield. The unusual two-storey building containing the booking office, which is entered at the upper level, has survived but the small shelter and footbridge were replaced when the line was electrified. In the background is the prominent Hunton Hill road bridge.

Erdington

Class '45' diesel-electric No. D80 at Erdington around 1972, on the 1V72 Sundays Only 08.30 Leeds City-Penzance. No. D80 became No. 45113 under TOPS in October 1973 and remained in service until 1988. Note the maroon enamelled running-in board is still in place.

A pair of Class '24s' headed by No. D5086 waiting at Erdington around 1969, probably on an excursion or possibly a Sutton Coldfield Motorail train, although these were diagrammed for a Type 4. The Class '24' has the early version of BR blue with the double arrows under the cab windows and the number on the body side. The diesel was renumbered as No. 24086 in 1974 and was withdrawn in January 1976 with collision damage.

Chester Road

Class '2P' 4-4-0 No. 40633 near Chester Road on a train to Birmingham, probably in late 1950 or early 1951. *The Railway Observer* reported in 1951 that this was a Burton shed working, starting with the 6.50am Burton-Walsall-New Street (arr. 8.19am), then the 8.50am New Street-Sutton Coldfield-Derby (arr. 10.53am). Next was the 12.53pm Derby-Sutton Coldfield-New Street (arr. 2.39 pm) and finally the 6.00pm New Street-Sutton Coldfield-Burton (arr. 7.34pm). No. 40633, which was fitted with Dabeg feed water apparatus, was recorded on this turn on several occasions and was withdrawn from Burton in 1955.

Ivatt '2MT' 2-6-2T No. 41320 on a Four Oaks-Birmingham working near Chester Road in 1955. No. 41320 had been transferred to Monument Lane in April 1955 to work the service and left for Watford at the end of March, when the diesels took over. The scene is almost unrecognisable today, with housing all the way up the line as far as Sutton Coldfield.

No. 41320 at Chester Road with a Four Oaks to New Street rail motor train on 3rd March 1956, the last day of steam operation. The L&NWR-built wooden station building did not survive modernisation in the 1980s. (Robert Darlaston)

Sutton Coldfield

The Stephenson Locomotive Society's 'Sutton Coldfield Centenary Special & West Midlands Rail Tour' train of 2nd June 1962 departed from Birmingham New Street at 2pm to Sutton Coldfield, where it reversed as shown in this picture. It next went to Stechford via Aston, back to New Street and then took the L&NWR Soho Loop line, on to Bescot, the Princes End Branch, Tipton, Smethwick and back on the Circle line to New Street. If that wasn't enough, the participants then transferred over to a DMU going to Bournville, along the canal branch to Lifford and Kings Norton, Halesowen, Old Hill, Stourbridge Junction and up to Wolverhampton Low Level, before returning via Walsall, Water Orton and Saltley for an arrival back at New Street at about 9.30pm! Ex-L&NWR 'G2' 0-8-0 No. 48930, which took the first half of the tour, was at Bescot from August 1956 until withdrawn in December 1962.

No. 48930 with the SLS special train to celebrate the centenary of the Sutton line on 2nd June 1962. It was originally advertised as 'Seven Hours with a Super D' but in the event the steam haulage was somewhat less than this. The train stands in the bay platform and the sharply curved through lines to Lichfield are on the right. Sutton Coldfield was the scene of a horrific accident in January 1955, when a Stanier Class '5' on a York to Bristol express, which was diverted from its normal route through Tamworth, came off the track because it was travelling at twice the 30mph speed permitted through the station. Sutton Coldfield Town Hall is in the background. (Robert Darlaston)

An arsonist caused considerable trouble in Sutton Coldfield in the early 1970s. The buildings on the Lichfield platform at Sutton Coldfield were destroyed on 3rd August 1972. Other stations were also damaged and several timber buildings in nearby Sutton Park were raised to the ground but the culprit was never traced. This photograph of the remains of the buildings at Sutton Coldfield was taken the day after the attack. (Robert Darlaston)

Four Oaks

Ivatt '2MT' 2-6-2T No. 41224 waits in the bay at Four Oaks with a motor train for Birmingham New Street on 27th February 1956, the last week of steam operation. It was one of three transferred to Monument Lane in April 1955 specially for this service and when the diesel units took over it was reallocated to Ryecroft. (Robert Darlaston)

The old and the new at Four Oaks; No. 41320 with its push-pull set and a Derby 'Lightweight' two-car DMU which is getting all the attention from the schoolboy spotters. This would be a pre-service test run as, after 4th March 1956, steam completely vanished from the line (except for Sunday diversions of Sheffield -Bristol trains). There was no transition period with steam helping out diesels. Not until the hard winter of 1963 did steam return to local services when for a while the 5.45pm New Street-Lichfield was worked by a 'Britannia'.

A Derby 'Lightweight' in the bay at Four Oaks on 10th March 1956, during the first week of the diesel service. The destination blind reads 'Four Oaks' rather than 'Birmingham New Street', so it is to be hoped that the driver who is just taking his seat remembered to change it before departure. The sidings on the right, where a carriage from the steam hauled service is stabled, have in recent years been built over with a block of apartments, the occupants of which will certainly have a good view of the trains on the 'Cross-City' line. (Robert Darlaston)

The Derby 'Lightweight' units were delivered brand new to Monument Lane depot for the start of the diesel service from Birmingham to Lichfield. Driving Trailer Composite No. M79649 leads on a Lichfield to New Street at Four Oaks on 10th March 1956, the first week of the new trains. (Robert Darlaston)

Derby 'Lightweight' Motor Brake Second No. M79134 waits in the bay platform at Four Oaks in 1956. It was delivered to Monument Lane during w/e 10th March 1956. The 'Lightweights' worked the service until the start of the 1958 Summer Time Table, when they were replaced by Metropolitan-Cammell three car units, later Class '101', which were of stronger and heavier construction. Over six hundred of these latter vehicles were built in its Birmingham factory within a four year period.

Brand new and still with white tyres, Driving Trailer Composite No. M79654 leads a four-car set comprising two of the Derby 'Lightweight' two-car units at Four Oaks in 1956. It was possibly on a crew training run prior to the start of the new service from Lichfield to Birmingham, given the blank destination board and the attention it is receiving from the locals. The station served one of the most prosperous suburbs of Birmingham, hence the two advertisements on the right for the Daily Telegraph, which cost just 2d at this date. This view shows both of the wooden ex-L&NWR station buildings, of which only the one on the left survives today.

The totems have been displaced by plain white signs and new lighting has been installed but the L&NWR signal box at the Birmingham end of Four Oaks station is still in use. The main station building on the Lichfield platform has gone, replaced by a typical 1970s 'bus shelter', whilst the goods yard is now overgrown and will soon become the station car park.

The waiting room and ticket office on the Birmingham platform at Four Oaks is still in use today as one of the authors can testify – his daughter is a regular traveller on the line to Birmingham. The passenger numbers are significantly higher nowadays compared with when this picture was taken in the early 1970s. A diesel multiple unit is in the bay platform and others are stabled behind.

Shenstone

No. 42668, seen at Shenstone on what is probably an excursion, was one of the last Stanier '4MT' 2-6-4Ts, built in November 1942 and allocated to Stoke. It had been loaned to Ryecroft shed at Walsall for a month in January 1949, which explains its presence here.

Shenstone station in the late 1960s, looking towards the Lynn Road overbridge in the direction of Lichfield. The 1884 building was very flamboyant and extensive for what was then a small village station on a secondary line. Unlike most of those at the other stations on the route, it survives virtually unchanged to this day on the electrified line and, indeed, is busier than ever as Shenstone itself has expanded significantly. Note that the platform had been raised to modern standards requiring a drop to the station doors.

Lichfield

A Derby 'Lightweight' unit heading for 'Birmingham via Aston' arrives at Lichfield City from the Trent Valley direction. This must be one of the early batch of units which did not have the 'yellow whiskers' below the front cab windows, unlike the later ones delivered in February/March 1956. On the left, the goods yard is still in use and original L&NWR gas lamps, complete with their tiny finials, still light the station.

Further down the platform at Lichfield City another early Derby 'Lightweight' prepares for departure to Birmingham. There are lots of officials in discussion, whilst the driver appears to be fault finding in the cab. The maroon enamelled signboards to the left show departures to Trent Valley and Derby from the other platform, and Sutton Coldfield, Birmingham, Walsall and Wolverhampton from where the DMU is standing.

A 'Compound' 4-4-0 with steam to spare, No. 41058 in March 1953 at Lichfield Trent Valley High Level, in a picture taken from beside the West Coast main line which runs underneath. The Gloucester Barnwood allocated engine still has 'LMS' on its tender, although the engine is in British Railways lined black.

Ivatt '2MT' 2-6-2T No. 41213 pictured at Lichfield City was allocated to Walsall Ryecroft from February 1955 to June 1958 but eventually ended up in Devon, on the Southern Region at Barnstaple in 1963. There is a very strong probability it was working a Walsall-Lichfield City turn, the 1.59pm from Walsall, returning from Lichfield City (SX) at 4.44pm to Wolverhampton High Level. On Saturdays, the train went through to Lichfield Trent Valley station, and then returned as Empty Coaching Stock to City.

A Park Royal DMU bound for Wolverhampton High Level is about to leave Brownhills station on the ex-L&NWR Walsall to Lichfield line in May 1959. This view looking north east was taken from High Street, a suffix applied to the station name between 1924 and 1930. The station remained in operation until 1965.

Class '45' No. 101 in the early 1970s at Lichfield City, coming off the line from Walsall. Train reporting number 8D49 was the 15.40 WSX Pensnett-Toton, which would account for the 21-ton hopper wagons making up the train.

The Sutton Park line (Castle Bromwich to Walsall)

After much argument about its construction through the middle of the magnificent Sutton Park, today a Site of Special Scientific Interest and designated in 1997 a National Nature Reserve, the Midland Railway opened its line from Castle Bromwich on the Birmingham to Derby main line to Ryecroft at Walsall in 1879. In addition to its local passenger and freight services, the route was used by excursions and trains diverted when engineering work was being carried out elsewhere in the Birmingham area. The Midland Railway provided an alternative to the L&NWR Walsall-Birmingham service with ten trains each day by 1922 but

these were cut-back to six in 1941 and, by 1950, were reduced to four each weekday, which continued until closure. For a time in the 1950s, there was an hourly service on Sunday afternoons in the summer between Walsall and Sutton Park only. The passenger service was scheduled to cease on 31st October 1964 but, because a replacement bus service from Aldridge had not been provided, it was reprieved until 18th January 1965. The line is still open today and carries a large amount of freight traffic which avoids the congested central Birmingham area.

Park Royal two-car DMU No. M56178 on a Birmingham to Walsall via Penns service in 1963 at Bromford Bridge. The Sutton Park line branched off the Midland line to Derby about 2¼ miles further east, at Castle Bromwich, where the train would call.

Sutton Park

Sutton Park station was built for the large number of visitors to the Park and in anticipation of this it had an additional third platform to accommodate trains terminating there from the Birmingham

direction. The main station building was on the Up platform but there was also a large structure on the Down island platform, with Platform 3 serving both arrivals and departures.

Sutton Park station had a fairly plain appearance, probably because of the absence of platform canopies. One interesting point to note, however, is the station sign in the centre of the photograph, an unusual combination of a painted BR totem on a rectangular board. The parcels vehicle in the background is standing on the third platform road, which could be used for both arrivals and departures. In 1960, five Birmingham to Walsall trains called at the station on weekdays, with an additional one on Saturdays, although only four made the journey in the opposite direction. Other details are the removal of the notice boards and the 'Ladies Toilet over Bridge' chalked on the seatback. The 'Gents' sign has been taken down and leans against the end wall below the LM&SR standard pattern (L&YR derived) wall lamp.

Saltley Class '5' No. 44775 is backing across the Up line into the goods loop, possibly with the daily parcels train for the large Post Office sorting depot, which was built in the Second World War as a Forces Post Office alongside the yard and which is still used by the Royal Mail today, albeit it is no longer rail connected. Note the broken station window with a newspaper stuffed in to stop the draught. This picture was taken after No. 44775 had completed a General overhaul at Cowlairs Works in February 1964, as evidenced by the large 10ins cab numbers and SALTLEY (BIRMINGHAM) on the bufferbeam, L&NER style. It was built with a forward top feed boiler but Cowlairs had swapped this for a central top feed boiler, although it has kept its Self Cleaning apparatus according to the SC plate on the smokebox door. No. 44775 was transferred to Mold Junction in June 1965 and withdrawn in late 1967.

BR Sulzer Type '2' No. D5031 in the mid-1960s passing through Sutton Park with a Class '4' freight from the Bescot direction, which consists entirely of wooden containers loaded into open wagons. This was normally strictly against the rules and since they are not new, this must have been a special movement. The 1959 Crewe-built diesel has a 1A Willesden shedcode painted on the bufferbeam near its left hand buffer; it was transferred there in February 1963. The goods loop and shed can be seen on the left of the picture and on the right the signals controlling access to and from the third platform line.

A Park Royal two-car DMU forming the 12.20pm Birmingham New Street to Walsall, at Sutton Park on 31st October 1964. (Robert Darlaston)

Streetly

Ivatt '2MT' 2-6-2T No. 41220 at Streetly on 4th August 1957, on a special push-pull working to Walsall and Wolverhampton. This was a Sunday and the service was provided for the Boy Scouts' Jamboree in nearby Sutton Park. Over 200 special trains ran during the two weeks of the event, which attracted over 80,000 visitors between 1st and 12th August. No. 41220 was on loan to Walsall from Watford, one of a number of engines brought in to supplement the local motive power. Block posts were set-up at Sutton Park and Streetly to cope with the volume of traffic, with one home and one fixed distant on each line at both stations; the temporary signal cabin and ground frame can be seen on the right. Loudspeakers were installed and a pathway was built from the station directly into the park, passing under the road bridge archway that was used for a loop line in Midland Railway days; this is just visible to the left of No. 41220. The front coach of the train is marked 'Pull & Push' as was LM&SR practice and not the commonly used 'Push & Pull'. No. M24319, a 57ft post-war Period III Driving Trailer to Diagram 2122, was not built until 1950. (Michael Mensing)

Ivatt '4MT' No. 43022 and Class '5' No. 45403 arriving at Streetly on Sunday 4th August 1957, with the 7.35pm return excursion to Stockport carrying visitors from the Boy Scouts' Jamboree in Sutton Park. No. 45403 was from Manchester Longsight and presumably would take the train forward on its own when it reached Bescot. The 2-6-0 was on loan at Bescot for two weeks from Devons Road shed in London to help with the large volume of additional traffic. Another twenty-five engines were loaned to sheds in the Birmingham district during the period, with a mixture of tank engines, 2-6-0s, Class '5's and even two 'Jubilees'. Streetly handled traffic from the north west via Walsall; Sutton Coldfield from the south off the former L&NWR lines; and Sutton Park, with trains from both north and south off the former Midland Railway lines. One of the temporary home signals is visible above the tender of the Class '5'. (Michael Mensing)

A Park Royal two car DMU, with Driving Trailer Composite No. M56157 leading, departing from Streetly with the 6.54pm Walsall-Birmingham New Street on Saturday 25th July 1964. The area to the right of the picture is now occupied by a residential development comprising several blocks of high quality apartments, in what is now part of Little Aston in Staffordshire, the area to the left of the line remaining as Streetly. One of the authors, who lives a few hundred yards from where this picture was taken, finds it difficult to imagine that a station was actually on this site. (Michael Mensing)

Aldridge

A Park Royal two-car DMU, later Class '103', leaving Aldridge on the 1.10pm Birmingham New Street to Walsall on Saturday 7th March 1964. These units were the mainstay of the line up until the passenger service ceased in January 1965. Behind the recovered rail sections are three NCB internal use wagons, each with a large 'X' painted on. (Michael Mensing)

Aldridge station on 31st October 1964, with a Stanier Class '5' backing a freight into the sidings to allow the 1.46pm Walsall-Birmingham New Street DMU to enter the station. The line to Walsall Wood and Brownhills, which was closed to passengers in 1930, branched off to the right, just beyond the goods yard. (Robert Darlaston)

7 – Leamington to Birmingham

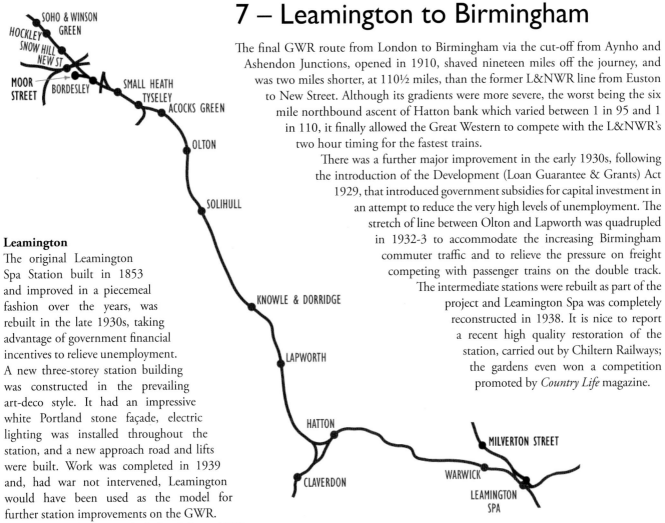

The final GWR route from London to Birmingham via the cut-off from Aynho and Ashendon Junctions, opened in 1910, shaved nineteen miles off the journey, and was two miles shorter, at 110½ miles, than the former L&NWR line from Euston to New Street. Although its gradients were more severe, the worst being the six mile northbound ascent of Hatton bank which varied between 1 in 95 and 1 in 110, it finally allowed the Great Western to compete with the L&NWR's two hour timing for the fastest trains.

There was a further major improvement in the early 1930s, following the introduction of the Development (Loan Guarantee & Grants) Act 1929, that introduced government subsidies for capital investment in an attempt to reduce the very high levels of unemployment. The stretch of line between Olton and Lapworth was quadrupled in 1932-3 to accommodate the increasing Birmingham commuter traffic and to relieve the pressure on freight competing with passenger trains on the double track. The intermediate stations were rebuilt as part of the project and Leamington Spa was completely reconstructed in 1938. It is nice to report a recent high quality restoration of the station, carried out by Chiltern Railways; the gardens even won a competition promoted by *Country Life* magazine.

Leamington

The original Leamington Spa Station built in 1853 and improved in a piecemeal fashion over the years, was rebuilt in the late 1930s, taking advantage of government financial incentives to relieve unemployment. A new three-storey station building was constructed in the prevailing art-deco style. It had an impressive white Portland stone façade, electric lighting was installed throughout the station, and a new approach road and lifts were built. Work was completed in 1939 and, had war not intervened, Leamington would have been used as the model for further station improvements on the GWR.

Leamington's engine shed dated from 1906, when a standard straight four road shed design was built following a fire in 1902 which destroyed the previous building. There was also a new brick-built coaling stage, with a 45,000 gallon tank on top and a larger turntable. The shed was coded 84D from January 1948 to August 1963 and 2L from September 1963 until it was closed in June 1965.

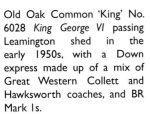

Old Oak Common 'King' No. 6028 *King George VI* passing Leamington shed in the early 1950s, with a Down express made up of a mix of Great Western Collett and Hawksworth coaches, and BR Mark 1s.

An immaculate 'Hall' 4-6-0 in lined BR black, No. 6924 *Grantley Hall*, sets off with a southbound train from Leamington Spa. In the background are the distinctive spires of the nearby All Saints Church. No. 6924 was allocated to Leamington for two years from the end of 1950, so this picture was probably taken during that time.

The signal is off for one of Leamington's own '5101' 2-6-2Ts, No. 5184, in 1956. The engine left for Gloucester Horton Road in 1962.

In their early days, the massive Churchward '47xx' 2-8-0s were quite rare on daytime freights and even here, the light seems to be fading as No. 4702 takes a heavy load northbound through Leamington Spa in 1956. Their heavy axle loading weight confined them to the Wolverhampton and Plymouth routes.

Churchward '43xx' 2-6-0 No. 6331 in 1956, on a Down local with a 'Fruit D' van ahead of its three coaches. It was allocated to Banbury from late 1955 until withdrawn in 1959. Leamington Spa General generated substantial passenger revenue for the Western Region; in addition to 3,700 season tickets there were 368,000 tickets issued annually in 1955.

The driver of 'King' No. 6006 *King George I* waits for the guard to give the right-away from Leamington Spa in around 1960. It must be August Bank Holiday – the boy with his dad is wearing a balaclava!

'Castle' No. 5001 *Llandovery Castle* at Leamington on 11th June 1962. Its appearance is not helped by the double chimney fitted a year earlier and its third different Hawksworth flat sided tender; this one was acquired in July 1961. These tenders were introduced during the Second World War with the 'Counties' and the 'Modified Halls' but subsequently found their way behind a number of the earlier engines. No. 5001 was allocated to Old Oak Common when pictured and remained there until withdrawn in 1964.

One of many 2-6-2Ts to be seen on shed at Leamington, No. 4171 on 11th June 1962. It had been transferred there from Tyseley in October 1954 and, like its classmates, was a regular on the local suburban trains in the area.

'Castle' No. 5076 *Gladiator* about to depart from Leamington Spa on the '1O46' Saturdays Only express, the 10.31am from Birmingham Snow Hill to Hastings, on 29th August 1962. The train consists of Southern Region green liveried coaches marked with set number '541'. No. 5076 was originally named *Drysllwyn Castle* but was renamed in January 1941 after the Second World War Gloucester Gladiator biplane. It was allocated to Reading from March 1960 until May 1963 and was paired with a Hawksworth tender during a Heavy Intermediate overhaul completed in May 1962.

Another 'Castle', No. 5085 *Evesham Abbey*, on the same day, with another set of green coaches, this time on '1V82', the 9.25am from Margate to Wolverhampton Low Level, where it was due to arrive at 3.51pm. No. 5085 was built in July 1939 using the frames from withdrawn Churchward 'Star' No. 4065, also taking its name. *Evesham Abbey* had been in store at Bristol St. Phillips Marsh since February 1962 but was reinstated at Reading shed on the 11th of August, presumably to help out with the summer 'extras'.

No. 6005 *King George II*, also on 29th August 1962, sets off past Leamington South Signal Box with a Birkenhead to Paddington express. Along with the rest of the class its days were numbered and it was withdrawn in October 1962. There would not be many more opportunities to take pictures like these three.

The 'Warship' class diesel-hydraulics were infrequent visitors to the West Midlands in the early 1960s. No. D817 *Foxhound* is about to depart from Leamington Spa on 4th August 1962. Along with No. D819, it was employed on the London-Wolverhampton route during August for crew training, in preparation for use as a substitute in the event of failure of the new 'Western' Class diesels on the accelerated Paddington to Wolverhampton services which were introduced with the 1962 Winter Time Table.

No. 6930 *Aldersey Hall* sets off from Leamington Spa General on 28th August 1962. It is on the connecting line from the LM&SR station, so has probably taken over an excursion. Leamington South Signal Box was first opened in June 1902 and closed in the late 1960s. Behind the box was the former L&NWR line from Leamington Spa Avenue to Rugby, that ran parallel to the GWR lines for some distance, separating at the site of the GWR shed.

Brush Type '4' No. 1747 with the 08.19 Paddington to New Street train in 1972. Note the platform still has its huge cast iron Great Western Railway running-in board, albeit now with a white background, and 'Passengers must not cross the lines except by the Subway' signs in place. The locomotive subsequently carried three different numbers under TOPS before it was taken out of service at the end of 1999.

Hatton

Hatton was the junction for the 9½ mile long branch to Stratford-upon-Avon and was built on a short level stretch just before the top of the six mile climb from Warwick. In 1897, the junction was made into a triangle by putting in the north curve, which enabled southbound trains to Stratford-upon-Avon and beyond to avoid reversing at Hatton.

In May 1914, the Down goods line was lengthened to cover the final 2¼ miles of the upward incline, extending it from Budbrooke to Hatton. The Working Time Tables set out the maximum permitted loads for various types of freight trains hauled by each power grouping of engines, with the '47xx' and '28xx' 2-8-0s in the highest 'E' group and 'Halls', 'Granges', '43xx' and '56xx' in the 'D' group. All were increased by fifty per cent when banking engine assistance was provided. One 2-6-2T was employed on banking and shunting at Warwick from 5.00am each day.

A very unusual class of engine on an unusual working at Hatton on 23rd July 1955. 'Dukedog' 4-4-0 No. 9022, which was allocated to the Cambrian Coast shed at Machynlleth, is passing through on the 7.35am Yaxley-Hatton brick train. It would have come from Peterborough via Rugby and Leamington, on what was normally a Stanier 2-8-0 duty. No. 9022 may have been commandeered off the 10.45am Leamington-Bordesley freight, a duty for which the 4-4-0 may well have been better suited. It is possible that it may have been working in the West Midlands following a visit to Wolverhampton Stafford Road Works where, apart from one wartime repair at Swindon, it had always been overhauled. (Robert Darlaston)

'Castle' No. 5012 *Berry Pomeroy Castle* working the 9.30am Bournemouth West to Birkenhead in 1955, seems to be making very light work of the five mile climb at 1 in 110 of Hatton Bank. It was allocated to Oxford shed from the end of 1952 until withdrawn ten years later. The final digit of the train reporting number '965' appears to have been found at the last minute.

The fireman takes it easy as Oxley allocated 'Hall' No. 4997 *Elton Hall* makes plenty of smoke on Hatton Bank in 1957. It has one of the smaller 3,500 gallon tenders which were fitted to the early members of the class when built in the 1930s. Its train has a mix of former LM&SR and GWR stock, all still in 'blood & custard' colours.

'Grange' No. 6812 *Chesford Grange* drifts down Hatton Bank with a three coach local in 1959. It was well off its beaten track, having been shedded at Pontypool Road since 1956.

'Western' Class diesel-hydraulics took over the Paddington-North West services from the autumn of 1962, until displaced by Brush Type '4' diesel-electrics in 1964. No. D1010 *Western Campaigner* approaches Hatton with the 1.10 pm from Paddington to Birkenhead on 26th January 1963, during the severe winter of 1962-3. (Robert Darlaston)

Hatton station, looking Up on 6th August 1966, with a fine early GWR bracket signal complete with additional bracket and gallery for the shunting signal. The running-in board includes the words 'Change for the Stratford-upon-Avon line' and, appropriately, a single diesel unit for Stratford-upon-Avon waits in the platform. (Robert Darlaston)

Lapworth

The angler continues to concentrate on his line as the 9.00am Paddington to Pwllheli passes the canal reservoir at Lapworth behind a 'King' on 2nd September 1961. (Robert Darlaston)

No. 6011 *King James I* passes Lapworth with the 12 noon from Birmingham Snow Hill to Paddington, the 8.50am from Birkenhead, on 3rd March 1962. (Robert Darlaston)

Knowle & Dorridge

This is one of those stations which has changed its identity several times. Although the village of Knowle is about two miles distant from the station, it was initially named Knowle when opened by the Great Western Railway in 1852 but was changed to Knowle & Dorridge in July 1899. In 1968, it again became plain Knowle as part of a London Midland Region policy of eliminating 'double barrelled' names but, in 1974, took on its current identity of Dorridge to reflect the reality of its location. The station was extensively remodelled between 1932 and 1933, as part of the quadrupling of the Birmingham main line, with new platforms, station buildings and signal box being provided. The goods shed was demolished and the yard reduced to make way for the additional main lines, and a larger replacement goods yard and shed was constructed on the Birmingham or Up side of the station. The goods facilities were taken out in September 1968; the north goods yard became a car-train loading depot and the relief lines became storage sidings for the car-train traffic.

Swindon, no doubt reluctantly, painted many of its named mixed traffic engines in lined black until British Railways 'relented' and replaced the L&NWR style livery with Great Western style lined green. No. 5935 *Norton Hall* is seen crossing one of the matching pair of girder bridges at Knowle & Dorridge in the early 1950s, on a southbound parcels consisting of one van and three bogie vehicles. The new goods yard built in the 1930s can just be seen in the left background.

Class '5101' 2-6-2T No. 4171 from Leamington shed departs from Knowle & Dorridge displaying a light engine headlamp, instead of the correct local passenger train lamp, which should have been at the top of the bunker back. This was in accordance with occasional GWR custom and is commented on elsewhere. The local is leaving from the Up Relief platform, while on the right of the island is the Down Main platform. The main station building was out of picture to the right of the Up Main platform.

Class 43xx' No. 6366 is captured by more than one photographer as it runs through Knowle & Dorridge with a southbound express in around 1957. The 2-6-0 was at Oxley until February 1958, when it moved to Swindon. On the right is the original goods yard, which was replaced when the line was quadrupled in the 1930s, by new facilities at the Birmingham end of the station. The station yard is being used to store redundant GWR 'Toplight' coaches built in the first decade of the century.

Bentley Heath

'Castle ' No. 5053 *Earl Cairns* on a London bound express about to pass under the footbridge and over the level crossing on the Up main line at Bentley Heath on 15th April 1952. The second coach is a former GWR 'Cornish Riviera Express' Centenary stock restaurant car.

A '2251' class 0-6-0 in 1952 at Bentley Heath, on a weed-killing train heading towards Birmingham. The train is made up from redundant GWR tenders and the leading one is fitted with a Collett style cab for protection of the staff. Behind the chemical tanks is an ancient 6-wheeled GWR clerestory but this is not for braking purposes because a 'Toad' is at the rear of the ensemble. The Knowle & Dorridge North Goods Yard and shed is just visible in the right hand distance. These were built in 1932 during the quadrupling of the line to replace the original goods facilities at the south end of the station.

No. 6866 *Morfa Grange* near Bentley Heath on 27th April 1963. The 'Grange' was a long-time resident of Tyseley shed staying there until withdrawn in May 1965.

Olton and Solihull

Olton station opened in 1869 on the GWR's Oxford & Birmingham extension and had, for some sixty-seven years, a two platform configuration. It was never seen as a station of significant importance, not even warranting a goods yard until 1933 when it was rebuilt, in common with other stations approaching Birmingham, with two island platforms. It developed from a mainly rural outpost to become a busy commuter station. It was at one time a busier passenger station than Solihull and, in the mid-1950s, had the largest sale of season tickets on the Western Region but was later overtaken by Maidenhead. Olton had three signal boxes over the years, with the first located at the Leamington end of the Up platform. This box was replaced in January 1907 when the GWR installed passing loops to the west of the station and constructed a new signal box controlling the junction. The third signal box replaced the junction box when the station was remodelled in 1933 and was finally closed in 1969.

Class '41xx' 2-6-2T No. 4148 on the 9.30am Knowle & Dorridge to Birmingham Moor Street local, seen near Olton from the front of the DMU operating the 8.45 Stourbridge Junction to Leamington Spa local on 2nd August 1957. The tank had been allocated to Worcester since mid-1956, so its appearance on a Birmingham suburban train is not readily explained. (Robert Darlaston)

'Dukedog' No. 9008 in 1952 on the Down Relief near Solihull, possibly working the 11.45am Leamington-Bordesley Class 'K' freight. There were four 'Dukedogs', No's 9007-10, at Tyseley in 1947 but, by early 1952, No. 9007 had been withdrawn and No. 9009 had gone to Machynlleth. No's 9008 and 9010 stayed on until June 1952, when they both moved to Oswestry.

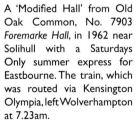

A 'Modified Hall' from Old Oak Common, No. 7903 *Foremarke Hall*, in 1962 near Solihull with a Saturdays Only summer express for Eastbourne. The train, which was routed via Kensington Olympia, left Wolverhampton at 7.23am.

Leamington shed's Class '5101' 2-6-2T No. 4171 in the mid-1950s at Solihull on an Up train, arriving from Birmingham and heading south towards Leamington Spa. It had been transferred from Tyseley in October 1954. No. 4171 was built by British Railways in October 1949, essentially to the same basic Churchward design from fifty years earlier. Note in the background the sheeted wagons which carried the car bodies and parts from Pressed Steel at Cowley to Rover at Solihull.

Class '5101' 2-6-2T No. 5194 from Leamington shed with a Down local at Solihull in the late 1950s. The 1930s rebuilding when the line was quadrupled left the stations along this route with a uniform appearance – the island platform buildings and canopies were of the same design at nearby Knowle & Dorridge, Acocks Green, Tyseley and Bordesley.

A type of 2-6-2T more usually associated with working on Paddington rather than Midlands suburban trains, Class '61xx' No. 6134, seen arriving at Solihull with an Up local, was at Tyseley from late 1953 until November 1957, when it moved to Leamington. The '94xx' 0-6-0PT is likely to be working the 9.15pm Morris Cowley-Longbridge that had been recessed at Solihull.

This picture of another 2-6-2T at Solihull was probably taken on the same day as that of No. 6134. The engine is wearing express passenger headlamps and is believed to be pulling an inspection saloon that appears to be one of the 809xx series, of which seven were built in 1948. They were kept in GWR chocolate and cream livery and all survive today in preservation, with two on the Severn Valley Railway.

'Prairie' tank No. 5101 waits for the signal at Solihull in September 1958. It had been transferred to Leamington from Stourbridge in July 1957 and stayed until withdrawal in 1963, and shows off a newly acquired coat of Great Western style lined green livery. It was the first new member of the class to be built for over twenty years, in November 1929, and could be distinguished by the outside steam pipes, and the reintroduced copper capped chimney and brass safety valve bonnets. The '5101's were an updated version of the '31xx' 2-6-2Ts, which had been renumbered into the '51xx' series between 1928 and 1930.

Acocks Green and South Yardley

Class '5101' No. 4108 at Acocks Green and South Yardley with the 2.50pm Birmingham Snow Hill to Lapworth local on 25th May 1957. The 2-6-2T was one of those built in the mid-1930s and was allocated to Wolverhampton Stafford Road at this date, but moved away to Newton Abbot the following year. (Robert Darlaston)

Tyseley

'Grange' 4-6-0 No. 6822 *Manton Grange* from Oxford passes through Tyseley station with a northbound freight in June 1959. It moved on to Cardiff Canton the following January and ended its days at Bristol Barrow Road, from where it was withdrawn in September 1964.

No. 1029 *County of Worcester* hurries through Tyseley on the 10.05am Wolverhampton-Kingswear, a Saturdays Only working, in 1962. The train is on the Up Relief Line and will take the North Warwickshire line to Stratford-upon-Avon. The Hawksworth 'County' was allocated to Swindon from August 1961 until it was withdrawn at the end of 1962. The GWR signage for its 'Express Goods Services – One Day Transits', although painted out, is still visible on the warehouse. On the left is the extensive carriage shed.

Tyseley shed

The Great Western Railway opened its Tyseley shed in 1908 at the same time as the North Warwickshire line, to replace a smaller shed at Bordesley. It had two standard roundhouses arranged side by side, one for passenger locomotives and one for freight, each having twenty-eight roads off its turntable, and a large twelve road heavy repair shop, known as 'The Factory'. Its allocation was mostly tank and mixed traffic engines, power for the London expresses being provided by Wolverhampton Stafford Road shed. A new DMU depot and storage sidings were built on parts of the site in 1957, to maintain the units introduced on the Birmingham area suburban and local services. The shed was taken over by the London Midland Region in January 1963, changing its code from 84E to 2A, and the freight roundhouse closed later that year. The next year, 'The Factory' was demolished and new diesel repair facilities built, and the steam shed finally closed in November 1966. All the buildings were demolished except for the coaling stage, which was leased to 7029 Clun Castle Limited and developed into today's Tyseley Locomotive Works and the base for Vintage Trains, the main line operating subsidiary of the Birmingham Railway Museum Trust.

Three local residents in one of the Tyseley roundhouses on 18th February 1962. On the left is No. 7808 *Cookham Manor*, which was there from January 1961 until October 1962, whilst on the right with its smokebox door open is No. 6926 *Holkham Hall*, which arrived in October 1961 and stayed until 1965. In the centre is No. 7918 *Rhose Wood Hall*, which was there from new in 1950 until withdrawn in 1965. Only the Western would continue to build engines to basically thirty year old designs as it did with both the 'Halls' and 'Castles'. It was certainly more economic than spending large sums designing new classes when existing designs did the job efficiently and economically.

Tyseley-based '57xx' 'Pannier' No. 3673 on 19th March 1961, in front of the two-road coaling shed which was later to form the kernel of the Birmingham Railway Museum. The 0-6-0PT remained allocated here until withdrawn in May 1964.

Hawksworth 'County' No. 1011 *County of Chester* has neither smokebox nor shed plate but is still in service with all its other plates. This photograph, with the DMU depot at a higher level on the right, was probably taken in September 1964 when the locomotive, as the only surviving 'County', was transferred to Tyseley to work a special organised by the Stephenson Locomotive Society. In the days prior to the special, No. 1011 was used on local services including the 5.45 pm Snow Hill to Henley-in-Arden, Stratford, Evesham and Worcester.

The elegant form of a Western Region 'Blue Pullman' set stretching out from Tyseley DMU shed on 18th February 1962.

A typical pre-1974 Health & Safety Act scene, with a loose wooden plank used to cross the inspection pit and a large pool of spilt oil. The pipe under the raised skirting is connected to the engine block coolant filler/drain valve. The radiator filler/drain valve is to the right of the cab step, directly above the vertical speedometer cable. The other two skirtings have been raised to enable the battery boxes to be pulled out for battery maintenance. BR Sulzer Type '2' No. D5023 had been transferred to Bescot from Camden in December 1965 and remained in the D02 Birmingham Division until June 1967. Renumbered under TOPS to No. 24023, it was withdrawn in September 1978 after less than twenty years in service.

Small Heath and Sparkbrook

A 'Castle', probably No. 5015 *Kingswear Castle* from Stafford Road shed, passing northwards through Small Heath & Sparkbrook in the mid-1950s on 'The Cornishman', which ran from Penzance to Wolverhampton. The two island platforms resulted from the quadrupling of the line in 1912-3; the one on the left served the Up and Down main lines and the one on the right the Relief lines, with the Down and Up Goods on the extreme right of the picture.

8 – The North Warwickshire line (Birmingham Moor Street-Stratford)

The North Warwickshire line ran from a junction at Tyseley on the Birmingham-London main line to Bearley West Junction, where it met the branch from Hatton to Stratford-upon-Avon and Honeybourne. Construction began in September 1905 and the 17¾ mile long line opened in December 1907 for goods and in July 1908 for passenger traffic. It had been promoted by the Birmingham, North Warwickshire & Stratford-upon-Avon Railway but that concern got into difficulties and it came under the control of the Great Western. The line not only opened up the south western suburbs of Birmingham but it also gave the GWR a new route from Birmingham to Bristol which was only 95 miles long, over thirty miles less than the shorter of the two existing routes. It joined the newly doubled line between Bearley, Stratford-upon-Avon and Honeybourne, where it met the new line between Honeybourne and Cheltenham which had been completed in August 1906.

In 1911, the GWR introduced four sets of coaches specifically for the Birmingham suburban traffic, each consisting of two First/Third Composites and two Brake Thirds. More new suburban stock was delivered in 1924, with seven permanently coupled four-coach sets and a further seven sets with conventional couplings in the following year. The staple motive power was the '41xx' 2-6-2T, a new batch of which was delivered to the Wolverhampton Division between 1929 and 1931. The service continued without any more major changes until September 1954 when the Western Region Winter Time Table introduced an intensified hourly regular interval service throughout the Birmingham area. These services were designed so that they could be turned over to diesel multiple units when they became available. This happened in June 1957, when Derby-built high-density three car units, later Class '116', took over most of the Birmingham suburban services.

The remaining services from Snow Hill to Bristol and to South Wales via Stratford were diverted to New Street from 10th September 1962. A new twice-daily DMU service was introduced on that date from Leamington Spa to Gloucester (via Hatton and Stratford) and lasted until May 1968 when closure notices for the North Warwickshire Line were published. Fortunately, the closure procedure was botched and, following a successful legal battle in 1969, the line remained open. Today, it hosts an hourly interval service from Stratford via Snow Hill to Stourbridge.

Moor Street

When Snow Hill station was rebuilt in the early 1900s, it was not economic for the Great Western Railway to widen the two track tunnel entering the station from the south, in the way that its northern approaches were improved. Consequently, Moor Street was built at the south end of the tunnel to reduce the traffic passing through and to handle local commuter traffic originating from Leamington and the new North Warwickshire line. The original intention had been to provide only a passenger station but when the opportunity arose to purchase adjacent land, a large goods depot was added. The first Moor Street terminus was opened in July 1909, although the station we know today was only brought in to use in January 1914 after the completion of extensive engineering works to increase the capacity of the approach lines and to construct the goods depot.

The station consisted of an island platform about 700 feet long, with the goods depot on three levels but a third platform was soon added as the island platform proved inadequate. There was a high-level yard primarily for perishable market traffic, extending over the whole area between Moor Street and Allison Street, with a covered platform 400 feet long, and below it were two low-level sheds, one for metal traffic and the other for general goods. Traffic access to and from the high-level yard to the low-level sheds was by means of hoists, which lowered and raised wagons with their contents, and each shed had a traverser to move wagons between its sidings and capstans.

Moor Street also handled excursion traffic and its two, space-saving, electrically driven, 60ft locomotive traversers, provided in place of the usual cross-over roads for transferring engines of incoming trains to

Great Western 2-6-2Ts dominated the suburban services into Moor Street station for thirty years. Two of the later '5101' Class were there on 28th May 1957, No. 4173 with the 3.10pm to Henley-in-Arden and No. 4112 on the 3.20pm to Leamington Spa. Note the goods shed on the left. (Robert Darlaston)

the outgoing road, were large enough to handle a 'Castle'. These were removed in 1967 since they were no longer needed and the following year, after the Snow Hill Tunnel was closed, Moor Street was left with just a handful of local services. Goods traffic had declined from the late 1950s onwards and finally ceased in November 1972. The old terminus was closed in 1987 after the reopening of the line through Snow Hill Tunnel, when a new station was built on the through line and it became redundant. However, Moor Street was not finished and, in a repeat of the position a century earlier, the rebuilt Snow Hill had reached its capacity and so the old terminus was reconnected to the main line and the Grade II listed station building was restored to 1930s condition.

One of the ex-GWR Large 'Prairie' 2-6-2Ts, No. 3101, on one of the two locomotive traversers at Birmingham Moor Street, after arrival with a Down local train on 28th May 1957. The electrically powered traversers have long since been removed but otherwise the scene is little changed in 2013. No. 3101, which was withdrawn from Tyseley shed three months after this picture was taken, was one of five engines rebuilt in late 1938/early 1939, using the frames from engines of the '3150' Class, with new boilers and smaller 5ft 3ins coupled wheels. They were originally intended for use on banking duties but were actually used mainly on local passenger work, with No. 3103 going new to Leamington shed. (Robert Darlaston)

One of a class better known for working in the South Wales valleys, '56xx' No. 6668 is seen at Moor Street on 28th July 1960, leaving the traverser after working in the 6.25pm from Knowle & Dorridge. This was one of four '56xx' 0-6-2Ts which were transferred from Barry in 1953 (the others were No's 6614/20/69), along with six '61xx' 2-6-2Ts, to replace ten BR '2MT' 2-6-2Ts which had been at Tyseley since they were built in 1952. To the right of the large goods shed is one of the two wagon lifts giving access to the lower level storage area that extended below the station. (Michael Mensing)

Class '61xx' 2-6-2T No. 6139 passing Moor Street in the mid-1950s with empty stock, the first vehicle of which is a turn of the century GWR 'Toplight' Composite still in wartime brown, followed by more modern ex-GWR and British Railways coaches. No. 6139 was one of the six members of this class transferred to Tyseley in part replacement for the ten '82xxx' Class 2-6-2Ts, No's 82000-9, in 1953, staying there until November 1959, when it moved back to more familiar territory at Oxford. Note in the background one of the two wagon hoists used to take goods wagons down to the street level depot, along with a suburban train in Moor Street station and the goods shed beyond. The ECS train is about to pass over the L&NWR approaches to New Street, with the deep cutting walls visible in the foreground of this unusual view, before plunging into the tunnel through to Snow Hill station.

An unusual and unexpected visitor, Eastern Region 'A1' 'Pacific' No. 60145 *St. Mungo*, attracts a crowd to Moor Street on a murky Sunday 5th September 1965. The Warwickshire Railway Society 'Pennine Railtour' on the previous day had been booked for Gresley 'A4' No. 60034 but this developed a hot box whilst running-in from Darlington Works. Another 'A4', No. 60004, also newly ex-works, was substituted but it too ran hot and so No. 60145, which was at Leeds Neville Hill, was rushed down to Saltley in the early hours of 4th September to work the special. This train departed from Birmingham New Street and travelled via Derby and Sheffield to Leeds, where *St. Mungo* handed over to No. 4472 *Flying Scotsman*, which took the train on to Carlisle via the West Coast main line. The same engines covered the return journey, No. 4472 using the Settle & Carlisle route back to Leeds. The next day, 5th September, No. 60145 worked another Warwickshire Railway Society Railtour (1X82), which it was originally scheduled to work to Weymouth but it was taken off at Banbury and replaced by No. 7029 *Clun Castle*. No. 60145 worked the special back from Banbury to Birmingham Snow Hill. The engine travelled to Saltley for servicing and was returned home the following day.

Moor Street station on 2nd March 1972, with a Class '116' DMU for Henley-in-Arden, part of Tyseley set No. 506. Cars were formed into numbered sets for operating purposes, the allocations being made on a board in the Maintenance Supervisor's office at Tyseley Depot. The 'Rotunda' tower in the left background is roughly equi-distant from Moor Street and New Street stations. The tall building on the right with the 'Co-operative' sign was knocked down and replaced by the 'Pavilions Shopping Centre' in 1987. (Robert Darlaston)

A view through the ticket barrier and concourse at Moor Street on 2nd March 1972, with a train for Henley-in-Arden in Platform 2. The goods station is already closed but the building still survives at the right. The advertisements make interesting reading, with an all-inclusive 'Winterbreak Weekend in London' for £9.30 Second Class/£11 First Class (one for Collectors' Corner at Euston) and the very far-sighted 'Northern Rock for all!' – which unfortunately came true in February 2008. The timetable on the barrier shows that the station at this date was only open on weekdays; this photograph was taken on a Thursday. (Robert Darlaston)

Hall Green

Class '5101' 2-6-2T No. 4161 at Hall Green with the 5.15pm Moor Street to Henley-in-Arden train, on 28th August 1958. Built after Nationalisation in September 1948, it had only arrived at Tyseley in April from Merthyr Tydfil shed but soon left for Wolverhampton Stafford Road, in November 1958. No. 4161 has a single headlamp at buffer beam level, indicating a light engine, rather than in the correct position near the top of the bunker for a local passenger. For some reason this had been a GWR custom, evidently still maintained at Tyseley in 1958. It seems that this was a common practice due to laziness on behalf of the crew, it being easier to put one lamp in the lower position instead of climbing up the bunker. (Robert Darlaston)

This photograph of Class '47' No. 1701 was taken from the Shirley end of the station, under the road bridge, in around 1970; the crossover in the foreground was still in place in September 1969. The carriages are leaking steam from the heating and there are few leaves on the trees, suggesting the picture was taken in late autumn. The headcode indicates the diesel is working a special, probably an Adex or Mystex on to the Western Region via Honeybourne.

Shirley

Class '61xx' 2-6-2T No. 6139 departs bunker first from Shirley with a Birmingham to Stratford train. This was another of the six of this class transferred to Tyseley to replace the '82xxx' Class 2-6-2Ts in 1953. The BR Standards, No's 82000-9, which had been there since they were built, were transferred to Barry and Treherbert during September and October, and Tyseley acquired No's 6105/16/18/34/39/66, along with No. 6121, the first time that '61xx' tanks had been stationed in the Birmingham area. However, it is quite possible that No. 6121's transfer was only on paper and the engine never left 81A, as it was only allocated to Tyseley for one month.

Another of the Class '5101' 2-6-2Ts, No. 4127, on a Birmingham to Stratford local at Shirley, almost certainly in 1957. It had arrived at Tyseley from Birkenhead in April but was quickly transferred to Severn Tunnel Junction in October.

A '94xx' 'Pannier' made a change from the usual '41xx' or '5101', as here with No. 9432, seen near Shirley on 3rd May 1957 with a Stratford-Birmingham local. Built by Robert Stephenson & Hawthorn Ltd in November 1950, it was at Tyseley for the whole of its brief nine year working life.

Earlswood Lakes

Class '57xx' 0-6-0PT No. 3660, from Tyseley, pauses at Earlswood Lakes in June 1957 with a train for Stratford. The station was at the highest point of the line between Birmingham and Stratford-upon-Avon and the long incline from the south required heavily loaded trains to be piloted from the latter station. The main station facilities here at Earlswood Lakes, including the booking office, were situated in the Down platform building and it had a goods yard which remained open until July 1964.

Wood End

Class '81xx' 2-6-2T No. 8109, from Leamington shed, leaving Wood End Tunnel heading towards the station and then Birmingham in June 1957. It moved to Tyseley in November 1960 and was withdrawn from there in June 1965, the last survivor of the class of ten. This view of the tunnel from the footpath on the embankment at the end of the Up platform shows the sharp curve of the tunnel bore. It is strange that the GWR did not continue the cutting for a short distance as this would have been a cheaper option than a tunnel.

Wood End Platform was opened on 1st July 1908, when the line was first opened for passenger traffic and had two platforms 400 feet long with shelters. The suffix 'Platform' was removed in July 1924 when it became known simply as Wood End. The station was just over eight miles from Tyseley Junction and located at the bottom of a cutting over 50 feet deep. It was immediately adjacent to Wood End Tunnel, the only significant engineering structure on the North Warwickshire line. A '51xx' 2-6-2T pauses at Wood End with a train from Birmingham. Unusually, it includes a fitted short wheelbase ventilated van as the leading vehicle. The station sign at this end of the platform was a very non-standard affair, consisting of a small board with beaded edges, the name being simply painted on. All the other signs were of standard GWR design.

Danzey

Class '5101' 2-6-2T No. 4172 waits at Danzey in June 1957, with the 3.26pm Birmingham to Stratford train. Built by British Railways in October 1949, it had been at Tyseley since March 1952 and stayed there until mid-1963. The mature 'GWR pine trees' form an attractive backdrop, as they did at so many stations by this date.

Probably no rail closure was avoided by so narrow a margin as that of the North Warwickshire line. The last trains were scheduled to run on Saturday, 3rd May 1969. Robert Darlaston made a 'final trip' on the line after leaving his office in Colmore Row, Birmingham on Friday afternoon, 2nd May, and photographed this DMU at Danzey. Passengers and staff were all in a sad, farewell frame of mind. However, that afternoon, an appeal by four local authorities to restrain British Rail from closing the line was heard in the Appeal Court by three Law Lords. They found against British Rail and were very critical of the 'unattractive conduct' of its practices. By the time Robert was on his way back to Moor Street, the news was out and blackboards were displayed on the platforms with the message 'Closure plans cancelled: see you all on Monday as usual'. It was 1984 before British Rail applied to have the injunction lifted but, in the meantime, attitudes to the subsidy of local rail services had changed and so, happily, passenger services on the line are now probably busier than ever before. Had the North Warwickshire line closed, Stratford would only have had a handful of peak-hour through services to Birmingham and at all other times a change of trains at Hatton would have been required, often with quite a long wait there. (Robert Darlaston)

Henley-in-Arden

One of the '81xx' series 2-6-2Ts, No. 8108, is seen at Henley-in-Arden in June 1957. Opened in 1908, the station consisted of three platforms, two formed by an island on the Up side and the other, containing the main station facilities, on the Down line. The island platform was accessible only to traffic from the north and was used mainly for originating and terminating services to Birmingham, although in earlier years it had also been used by trains for the Lapworth Branch.

Another view on the same occasion. The ten '81xx' 2-6-2Ts were rebuilt using the frames from withdrawn '51xx' engines in 1938-9. It had been intended to complete fifty but the remainder were suspended when war broke out. They had new front ends and boilers, and 5ft 6ins coupled wheels to improve acceleration on suburban passenger work. No. 8108, which was rebuilt from No. 5133 in September 1939, was shedded at Tyseley. This view of the Birmingham end of the Down platform shows the porter's summer house in the background. The overhead wire suspended between the lampposts on the Down platform is linked to the signal box, which is to the left off camera.

Wilmcote

Fowler '4F' 0-6-0 No. 44247 from Northampton shed in August 1961, at Wilmcote en route home via the lines of the erstwhile Stratford-upon-Avon & Midland Junction Railway (S&MJR). Following the closure of Stratford S&MJR shed, locomotives working that line were stabled at Stratford GWR shed. The '4F' may have been 'borrowed' to pilot a Down train from Stratford and was returning, probably from Bordesley, with this Class 'H' through freight.

Stratford-upon-Avon

The Great Western station at Stratford was opened on its current site in 1861, replacing the terminus of the former Oxford, Worcester & Wolverhampton Railway line from Honeybourne and the terminus of the Stratford Railway Company's branch line from Hatton. It was rebuilt in 1907 as part of the upgrading of the line from Bearley to Honeybourne, on the Great Western's new main line route to the West of England. Stratford had a Great Western engine shed built to the Churchward standard straight road design, with a combined coaling stage and water tank but no turntable, which was opened in 1911 as a sub-shed to Tyseley. It was closed in September 1962.

Ex-GWR railcar No. W29W at Stratford-upon-Avon on 7th October 1955. It was one of three based at Leamington, from where they worked a regular service to Stratford via Hatton. It is one of the later pattern units with buffers and drawgear, and lasted until August 1962. The coach coupled to the railcar is probably the through carriage from Stratford-upon-Avon to Paddington, which was attached at Leamington Spa to the 2.35pm from Birkenhead (6.00pm from Birmingham Snow Hill).

Diesel railcar No. W5W waiting to depart from Stratford on 7th October 1955; note the difference in front end styling from No. W29W. The rounded appearance of the earlier railcars led enthusiasts to christen them 'Flying bananas'. No. W5W had a body built by the Gloucester Railway Carriage & Wagon Co. but, as can be seen, it did not have conventional buffers and drawgear; it was withdrawn in December 1957.

No. 5015 *Kingswear Castle*, from Wolverhampton Stafford Road shed, at Stratford-upon-Avon in the late 1950s, probably on 'The Cornishman' given the pristine chocolate and cream liveried coaches. The 'Hall' appears to be hooking on – it was quite normal for trains leaving Stratford to be assisted up the long 1 in 75 towards Bearley (thereafter the climb to Earlswood continues at 1 in 150). 'Castles' were permitted to take 420 tons from Bristol as far as Stratford but were limited to 364 tons on to Birmingham.

Another Stafford Road 'Castle' heading for home, No. 5022 *Wigmore Castle* is seen departing northwards from Stratford on 'The Cornishman' in 1957. The train consists of an immaculate set of British Railways Mark 1 coaches in the newly re-introduced chocolate and cream livery; the headboard reads 'Wolverhampton-Birmingham-Bristol-Plymouth-Penzance'.

No. 2211, a Collett '2251' 0-6-0, the modernised 1930s version of the 'Dean Goods', at Stratford GWR shed on 15th May 1960. Its last two postings were Tyseley in June 1959 and Leamington in December 1960, from where it was withdrawn in late 1964. The depot was a sub-shed of Tyseley and *The Railway Observer* reported in 1953 that it had workings for five engines, three passenger and two freight. The passenger engines, '51xx' and '61xx' Class 2-6-2Ts, worked the local trains to Birmingham and the '2251' 0-6-0s were mainly used on banking and piloting duties on the severely graded Birmingham line. All except the shortest freights needed assistance and this continued into the 1960s.

Class '5101' 2-6-2T No. 4142, from Worcester shed, waits at Stratford on 15th May 1960. It moved to Gloucester Horton Road three months after this picture was taken and spent its final few months in service in South Wales, at Neath in late 1963.

'Castle' No. 7026 *Tenby Castle* sets off from Stratford-upon-Avon with the Down 'Cornishman' on 12th June 1962, passing Stratford West Signal Box. The condition of the Mark 1 coaches has deteriorated since the pictures on the previous pages were taken some five years earlier. (Robert Darlaston)

Enthusiast railtours often brought engines which would never normally be seen so far away from their home 'patch' and often used classes which were normally found only on freight work. Two such engines, from the Southern Region shed at Guildford, were Maunsell 'U' class 2-6-0 No. 31639 and Bulleid 'Q1' 0-6-0 No. 33006 which, on 7th March 1965, worked the Home Counties Railway Society's 'Six Counties Railtour'. This started at London Paddington and reached Stratford-upon-Avon via the S&MJR route. From there the train went via Leamington, Rugby and Northampton to Wellingborough, before returning to Paddington via Bedford, Fenny Stratford, Bletchley, Bicester and Oxford.

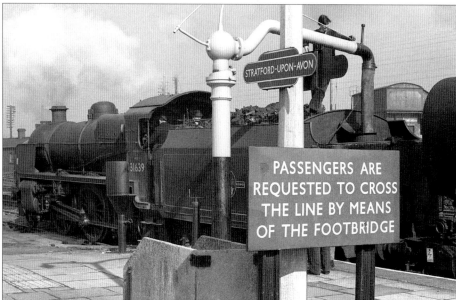

Above: The train arrives at Stratford-upon-Avon from the S&MJR Stratford Town station.

Left: The fireman of No. 31639 makes sure the tender tank is filled up.

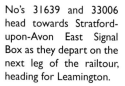

No's 31639 and 33006 head towards Stratford-upon-Avon East Signal Box as they depart on the next leg of the railtour, heading for Leamington.

9 – Birmingham Snow Hill

The Great Western Railway opened Snow Hill station in the 1850s, initially as a terminus and then, in 1854, as a through station, once the line to Wolverhampton through Hockley Tunnel was completed. The original temporary timber structure was rebuilt in 1871, at the same time as the broad gauge trackwork was converted to standard gauge. In 1905, the GWR decided to carry out a complete reconstruction of the station to cope with the increased volume of traffic it was now experiencing. The constraints of the site on both east and west sides forced the GWR to expand northwards, resulting in 1,200 feet long platforms. The new station had two Up and two Down lines, served by two island platforms and four bays at the north end. No bays were provided at the south end, because a decision had been taken to open a terminus for suburban traffic south of the city at Moor Street in 1909, to reduce the traffic using the double track tunnel, which could not be expanded because the cost would have been prohibitive. Scissors crossovers were employed half-way along to allow each platform to accommodate two trains, that could then arrive or depart independently and which led to the four main platforms each having two numbers, one for the south end and one for the north end.

Work was completed in 1912 and resulted in an impressive station with a new entrance and booking hall concourse spanned by an arched roof. Two thirds of the platform length was covered by a 'ridge and furrow' type overall roof, finished off by a glazed windscreen, with the other third having individual canopies for each platform. Distinctive salt glazed bricks set off by buff terra-cotta cornices, strings and copings were used to face the buildings. A new North Signal Box was opened in October 1909 and, because of the limited space available, it was built on a narrow steel gantry which overhung the lines on either side and with electrical operation of the points and signals. Unlike the constricted south end, the line towards Hockley was widened to four tracks to accommodate the increase in traffic.

The station suffered some bomb damage in the Second World War, although not as much as New Street, and the overall roof was re-glazed as a result. After that there was only routine maintenance and repainting, with new BR signage introduced in the early 1950s. When the rebuilding of New Street station and the associated electrification works started in 1959, the London Midland station lost its direct London trains, which were transferred to the Western Region route, increasing Snow Hill's from nine each way to fifteen Down and fourteen Up. However, this proved to be an 'Indian Summer' for Snow Hill and the writing was on the wall after the London Midland Region took over the Birmingham area of the Western Region on 1st January 1963. Once New Street was finished and the new electric services were operational in 1967, closure of Snow Hill was announced. All of its services were to be switched to New Street from 6th March and the tunnel to Moor Street was closed a year later. Local services north to Wolverhampton Low Level continued and there were four trains each day to Langley Green via Smethwick West, using Class '122' single car diesel units, but outright closure came on 4th March 1972.

The Snow Hill station frontage in Colmore Row, Birmingham on 27th March 1966. The impressive 'Passengers Entrance' is spoiled by the downmarket retail premises on either side, with a clearance shop and a bookmakers nearest to the camera. The rebuilding to create the third Snow Hill station started in 1906 and was completed in 1912. It included pedestrian access from Colmore Row into the new booking hall, formed by creating a new entrance as part of the former Great Western Hotel's façade. The hotel was taken out of public use and converted into office accommodation, partly because it was said that the noise and smoke of the trains passing underneath was, unsurprisingly, not popular with the guests. (Robert Darlaston)

Inside the booking hall at Snow Hill on 4th April 1966. The rebuilt station of 1912 had a large booking hall with an arched stained glass roof. The walls were in white imitation marble, which reflected light and was easy to keep clean. Vehicles accessed the area through the famous wrought iron gates now preserved at the Birmingham Railway Museum at Tyseley. Two of the seven ticket windows were originally for excursion traffic. Those to the right, numbered 1 to 5, were 'arranged alphabetically', according to the enamel sign between windows 2 and 3. In its prime, Snow Hill had three booking offices, the others being at the Great Charles Street entrance and on Platform 1 but a former member of staff who worked at Snow Hill in the 1950s only ever remembered the latter being used for paying staff wages. The large advertisements above the booking windows, promoting the 'Engineering & Building Centre in Broad Street', 'Deutsch & Brenner's Aluminium Extrusions' and 'Ascot Gas Water Heaters', together with the dangling wires, add to the overall air of shabbiness. There are car parking bays in the driveway area and road traffic is now directed around an island, which has two notices informing drivers that the car parking is limited to fifteen minutes for dropping off passengers. Hopefully the driver of the BMC 1800 has heeded the 'No Parking' notice. (Robert Darlaston)

Early 1950s

This picture, taken in around 1956, shows 'Castle' No. 5070 *Sir Daniel Gooch* assisted by a 'Dukedog' 4-4-0, the pilot being positioned behind the train engine in traditional Great Western fashion. The Stafford Road 'Castle' and its train have just emerged from Hockley No. I Tunnel and are passing the 1909-vintage North Signal Box. On the right against the 'Toad' brake van is a GWR diagram DC4 'Cordon' gas tank wagon, used to transport gas for carriage lighting and restaurant car cooking purposes.

Class '43xx' 2-6-0 No. 6365 from Gloucester Horton Road is shunting carriage stock into either New Yard or Northwood Street Sidings at the north end of Snow Hill; it had probably arrived on a train from Hereford. It was shedded there from July 1954 until withdrawn in late 1963, apart from a month at Oxley in summer 1955. Note that the turnout is equipped with a long detector bar.

An ex-ROD 2-8-0, No. 3029, on a loaded northbound iron ore train in 1955. It is likely to be the 12.55pm Banbury Oxfordshire Ironstone Company (OIC) to Bilston West, which was due to pass Snow Hill at 2.45pm. The Great Western Railway purchased twenty of these engines, which were closely based on a design by J.G. Robinson for the Great Central Railway, from the War Department in 1919 and hired a further eighty-four between 1919 and 1922. It then purchased eighty of them from the Government in 1925 and, in 1926-7, the best fifty were overhauled and renumbered, including No. 3029; the others were scrapped by 1931. No. 3029, which had been built by the North British Locomotive Company in 1925 and was originally numbered No. 3053, was withdrawn from Oxley shed in May 1956.

Class '14xx' 0-4-2T No. 1438 on a Birmingham to Dudley auto train at Platform 5 in 1956, this service being nicknamed the 'Dudley Dodger'. Dieselisation of most local services from Snow Hill started on 17th June 1957. No. 1438 was allocated to Stourbridge but moved away to Southall in November 1957. Stourbridge shed provided the motive power for Dudley-Snow Hill trains – either a '14xx' and autocoach or a GWR diesel railcar – because of the reversal at each end of the journey. The leading 70ft auto trailer is number W83W of Diagram 'U', built in 1912 with 70 seats. These did not have luggage space and had additional end entrance doors compared with those built for branch line work. It had been transferred from the Banbury area and is seen here in filthy maroon livery.

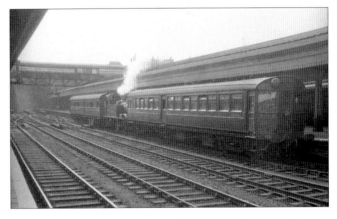

No. 1438 departs from Snow Hill past the North power box on its slender steel gantry which overhung the tracks on both sides. The 'Dodger' was usually just a single auto trailer, so probably this was a rush-hour service, with the locomotive 'sandwiched' between two trailers. The 70ft auto trailer nearest to the camera, a Diagram 'L' built in 1906, has had part of the beading plated over and is running on Collett 7ft bogies. It is likely to be either No. W44 or W45, which were both withdrawn in November 1957. No. 1438 with auto coaches was only used on the 'Dudley Dodger' if one of the ex-GWR diesel railcars was unavailable. Railcar No's 8 and 14 were the usual vehicles, being allocated to Stourbridge shed for most of the 1950s.

GWR railcars

There were several types of railcar amongst the thirty-eight built by the GWR before the Second World War. The first four were built by AEC in 1933-4, followed by the next three of an improved design by the Gloucester Railway Carriage & Wagon Company. Cars No's 2-4 were used on a completely new service from Snow Hill to Cardiff via Stratford until 1940, when they were replaced by the twin-units (cars No's 35-38) because of the increased traffic. From about 1941, the railcars were replaced by steam hauled carriages, because traffic had grown to require full length trains.

Next came three more variants of the design: six were similar to the previous three, three had toilet facilities and one was an express parcels vehicle. With the delivery of this series, the principle by which the Great Western operated its railcars was changed. Previously, the railcars were intended to supplement the existing steam traffic and in this they succeeded to the extent that they had to be replaced by steam hauled trains but, after the introduction of No. 18 with its standard buffers and drawgear enabling it to haul a trailing load, it was shown that railcars could transform a previous loss-making branch service and retain the ability to work the fast main line stopping services when required.

The GWR built the next batch of railcars in September 1938 but with the company producing the underframes, bogies, brake gear and bodies, and AEC supplying the engines and transmissions for construction at Swindon. Not all cars were alike, No's 19 to 33 were intended for branch line working, No. 34 was a second express parcels car, while No's 35 to 38 were designed as twin-sets, with buffets and toilets for working the Birmingham to Cardiff service.

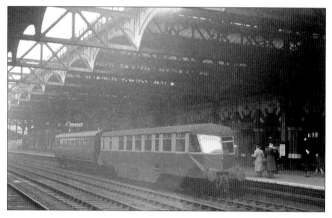

Although most of the Dudley local services were steam worked up until 1957, there had for many years been two scheduled daily trains which were operated by Stourbridge-based former Great Western Railway diesel railcars and these continued to work until the late 1950s. No. W25W is pictured in March 1953 after arrival at Platform 7, towing a GWR suburban brake coach to augment the passenger capacity. The later railcars with standard drawgear lasted longer than the earlier examples, No. W25W remaining in service until August 1962.

Diesel railcar No. W14W stands in No. 4 bay platform in 'blood & custard' livery, probably whilst working a Dudley service in 1958, on which it was a regular at this date. No. W14W had a 70-seat capacity and was powered by two AEC bus engines. Unlike No. W25W, it does not have conventional buffers and drawgear, and therefore could not work with a strengthening coach; it was withdrawn in August 1960.

Express Parcels diesel railcar No. W17W, seen coupled to a parcels vehicle and standing in Platform 10, is missing the figure 1 from its number. As with its passenger carrying peers, No. W17W used two AEC 8.85 litre engines with a gearbox fitted to each engine and had three pairs of sliding doors. It was painted in all over maroon in late 1952 but this picture was probably taken several years later. No. W17W was withdrawn in January 1959, when the new British Railways diesel parcels units came into service.

Interlopers from the London Midland Region

Stanier 'Coronation' No. 46237 *City of Bristol* was loaned to the Western Region between 23rd April and 21st May 1955, during which time it was used on Paddington to Wolverhampton and Birkenhead trains, as well as on the 'Cornish Riviera' between Paddington and Plymouth. The Western crews were unfamiliar with the engine and failed to get the best from it, and it did not produce anywhere near the typical day-to-day performances obtained by the London Midland Region from its big 'Pacific's. However, No. 46237 proved quite capable of taking normal Western Region loads on existing timings without difficulty despite the way it was worked.

In January 1956, after the Western Region 'Kings' were discovered to have serious problems with their bogies that required immediate attention at Swindon, two 'Coronation' 'Pacific's, No's 46254 and 46257, were sent to Old Oak Common from the London Midland Region. They were joined at the beginning of February by two 'Princess Royals' but the 'Kings' were soon coming back in sufficient numbers to release the LMR engines and they were returned before the end of the month. No. 46257 *City of Salford,* at Platform 5 alongside 'Hall' No. 5994 *Roydon Hall,* was on Train 180, the 9.10am Paddington-Birkenhead, which appears to be accurate in this picture, unlike the one below.

London Midland 'Princess Royal' No. 46207 *Princess Arthur of Connaught* entering Snow Hill during its three weeks on loan to the Western Region at Old Oak Common in February 1956, when the 'Kings' were taken out of service with serious bogie problems. Although the train is clearly running in a southbound direction, its train reporting number 180 was for the 9.10am from Paddington to Birkenhead. The balancing working was the 2.35pm from Wolverhampton to Paddington, which is presumably the train the 'Princess' was working in this photograph.

Western 1950s and 1960s

The Birmingham area 2-6-2Ts worked on freights as well as the suburban trains. Class '5101' 2-6-2T No. 4170, from Tyseley, is on a trip working at Snow Hill on 2nd June 1954. The October 1949-built engine was an early withdrawal, in September 1960.

The Western Region in its usual fashion repainted as many locomotives as possible in Great Western lined green including '5101' No. 4178, seen here waiting at Snow Hill with a local in 1962. Its shed plate is missing, which suggests this picture was probably taken after its transfer from Wellington to Stourbridge Junction in August and before its subsequent move to Leamington the following month. This engine has bunker side steps, whereas No. 4170 in the photograph above does not; these were a BR fitment and were not applied to all engines.

One of the less well-known members of the 'Castle' Class was Old Oak's No. 5035 *Coity Castle*. It was named after a ruined edifice near Bridgend, Glamorgan. No. 5035 was allocated to Old Oak Common throughout the 1950s, moving to Swindon in September 1960.

The Fridays Only Wolverhampton to Paddington was running a few minutes late as it arrived at Platform 7 in April 1961, behind No. 6017 *King Edward IV*. It was due to depart at 4.45pm but the crowds of people and luggage on the platform suggest it will be delayed further.

A classic Snow Hill scene as No. 6021 *King Richard II* arrives at Platform 7 with the 3 o'clock to Paddington, the 11.40am from Birkenhead, on 28th October 1961. The famous clock shows the train was a few minutes late; it had been held outside the station while a parcels van was removed from the rear of a preceding local. (Robert Darlaston)

One of the Collett 2-8-0s with side window cab, No. 3835, drags a southbound freight of ironstone empties, probably the 8.40am Bilston-Banbury OIC, which passed Snow Hill at 11.0am, up the incline from Hockley Tunnel in the late 1950s. These would be returning from the former Stewart & Lloyd's steelworks at Bilston to Wroxton, just north of Banbury, where the Oxfordshire Ironstone Co. had its extensive quarries. The 1942-built engine was shedded at Cardiff Canton between March 1957 and June 1960. To the right of the train were the New Yard Sidings and in the distance Northwood Street Sidings, where carriage stock was kept.

'Hall' No. 6926 *Holkham Hall* takes the Up through line in 1963, with a freight of indeterminate type, since the engine is carrying lamps for a light engine. It has a Hawksworth tender, swapped from one of the later 'Modified Halls', and was at Tyseley from September 1961 until transferred to Banbury in May 1965, where it was withdrawn almost immediately.

One of the earlier '57xx' 0-6-0PTs, No. 7713, with round front cab windows and single radius roof in 1958 on a trip freight passing Snow Hill North Signal Box. A pair of single bolsters lead the mixed freight; perhaps they had been carrying something oversize, hence the 'Toad' brake van behind them. No. 7713 was at Tyseley from May 1950 until August 1959. The North Signal Box was opened in 1909 and was taken out of use in 1960. It was one of the first all electric signalling systems on the Great Western Railway. The line to the immediate right of the signal box was a short spur siding and then came the two main lines.

Class '56xx' 0-6-2T No. 5679, running light northbound, was shedded at Stourbridge Junction from March 1963 until withdrawn at the end of July that year. The engine is using one of the scissors cross-overs to switch from the Down Through to the Platform line. These junctions were located on the north side of the plate girder bridge crossing Great Charles Street and allowed two short trains to enter and leave the main Up and Down platforms independently of each other. For this reason the single Up platform face was numbered platform 7 and continued as Platform 8, and the Down Platform 6 was continued as Platform 5.

One of the 'Panniers' built to replace the old GWR '2021' class in the 1930s, '74xx' No. 7426 leaves a smoke trail as it passes northbound through Snow Hill on a trip working. It arrived at Tyseley in March 1961 and was withdrawn just over two years later.

No. 6842 *Nunhold Grange* on the Down through road with a train of oil tanks, likely to be the 1.50am Acton to Oldbury & Langley Green fuel oil, which was due to pass through Snow Hill at 9.45am. It is 'heavy oil' and therefore no barrier vehicles were required. The 'Grange' was at Stourbridge Junction from September 1962 until April 1964, when it was transferred to Tyseley.

One of the final batch of 'Castles' built by British Railways No. 7022 *Hereford Castle* being 'cabbed' by several young spotters at Snow Hill in 1964. It had a double chimney fitted in December 1957, was paired with a Hawksworth flat sided tender from December 1961 and is seen with a replacement front smokebox number plate. It was shedded at Worcester between April and October 1964, and then moved to Gloucester Horton Road, from where it was withdrawn the following June. The tall building in the background with the 'S&L' sign is the thirteen storey Lloyd House, which opened in 1963 as the headquarters for the Birmingham City Police.

One of the later '57xx' 'Panniers', usually known as the '8750' Class, which had improved cabs with larger windows, No. 4646 is passing the 'Western Pullman' in Platform 5 as it trundles over the scissors crossover for the Up platforms. It was at Stourbridge Junction throughout the 1950s and was transferred to Tyseley in July 1966, only four months before withdrawal.

No. 4646 had lost its cast cab numberplates, which had been replaced by a passable painted imitation of the GWR serif pattern numerals. This engine was one of the last three former GWR standard gauge locomotives to remain in service with British Railways. 'Pannier' tanks No's 4646, 4696 and 9774 were all withdrawn together on 12th November 1966, the month when Tyseley closed to steam. Croes Newydd's No. 9641 had been withdrawn a week earlier but is rumoured to have continued in unofficial use for a short time after withdrawal.

With a painted 2B Oxley shed code, No. 6871, formerly known as *Bourton Grange* and seen here at Birmingham Snow Hill on 13th June 1965, was within four months of withdrawal and is running without nameplates, cabside plates or smokebox number. It is on a Class 'D' express freight at least thirty per cent of which is vacuum fitted. As can be seen, the canopy has been replaced and the scissors crossovers re-laid following the re-construction of the bridge over Great Charles Street in the summer of 1964.

London Midland takeover

Stanier '8F' No. 48680 brings a southbound freight out of Hockley Tunnel in late 1963. The 2-8-0, built for the LM&SR at the Southern Railway's Brighton Works in 1943, had moved from Northampton to Bescot in November 1962. In the right distance, a DMU is stabled in Northwood sidings and two more sets on the left are in the Platform 8 bay.

A long-time Saltley resident, '8F' 2-8-0 No. 48351 clanks through with a short southbound freight in late 1963.

Stanier Class '5' No. 44897 heads a fitted freight out of the south portal of Hockley No 1 Tunnel, past a DMU parked on the stub road which was in front of the old North Signal Box. The factory of Taylor & Challen Ltd, which made industrial presses, appears in the background of many pictures taken at Snow Hill. It was built of red brick with superb decorative stone and brickwork, which accorded it Listed Building status. The company's name was on a large panel of ceramic tiles in slightly scrolled Edwardian lettering, which is visible below the later signage. The Great Western 'Toad' brake van on the right, branded 'COND', seemed to be parked in this spot for many years.

No. 44897 has made its way through the station and is waiting to take its train through the southern tunnel. The Class '5' had been transferred from Mold Junction to Shrewsbury in April 1966. The advertisement above the loaded cattle van showed the Birmingham Theatre was hosting The National Dance Troupe of Sierra Leone, with their 'Pulsating Exciting Rhythms of Africa', commencing on Monday 20th June 1966.

The clock on Platform 7 shows 12.33pm as Stanier Class '5' No. 44762 is about to move off with its brake van into the tunnel towards Moor Street. The later pattern of Stanier tender, with part-welded tanks and oblong shaped vents on the rear bulkhead, shows up well. To its right are two interesting signs, the cream and brown circular station totem, a style found only at Snow Hill and Bristol Temple Meads, and one for the 'Rail Air Service'. No. 44762 was one of the last LM&SR-built Class '5's and was one of three painted in green in January 1948, when the newly formed British Railways was deliberating about the liveries it would adopt. It was at Tyseley from December 1965 until the following November.

The 'Birmingham Pullman'

The 1960 glossy brochure which accompanied their introduction began '*The British Transport Commission, as part of the Modernisation Plan, has decided to introduce de-luxe Pullman Diesel trains between important business centres.*' The streamlined fixed formation sets were air-conditioned, an important selling point since no other trains had this feature at the time, and were painted in a striking pale blue livery set-off by white around the double-glazed windows. British Railways introduced them on the London Midland and Western regions in an attempt to attract business travellers on three important routes to London. The former employed its sets on the London-Manchester service, while the latter put them on its West Midlands and Bristol business trains. They were built in Birmingham by Metropolitan-Cammell and those on the Western were eight car sets, with a mix of First and Second Class seats, whereas the London Midland six-car sets were all First Class; meals were served at all seats in the traditional Pullman manner.

The inaugural run of the 'Western Pullman' was on 12th September 1960, with the West Midlands train leaving Wolverhampton Low Level at 7.00am and calling at Birmingham Snow Hill, Solihull and Leamington Spa before arrival in London at 9.35am. The train returned as far as Birmingham in the middle of the day, leaving Snow Hill at 1.00pm before a final trip back to the Midlands, departing at 4.50pm and reaching Wolverhampton at 7.20pm. The train undoubtedly helped the railway retain its business travellers during the seven years that the London Midland service was disrupted by electrification works but when the new electric trains were introduced in 1967, they provided a standard service which rendered the Pullmans redundant. The 'Birmingham Pullman' ceased in March 1967, along with the other main line services to Paddington from Snow Hill.

The streamlined front end of the 'Birmingham Pullman' standing in Platform 7 contrasts with grubby Stanier '8F' No. 48680 in late 1963. Note the signs for each individual Pullman car and an unusual sign, 'Down', which has nothing to do with the trains but is an indication to passengers using the stairs to keep to one side for down and the other for up. The clock is coming up to the 1.00pm departure time; the train was due in at Paddington at 2.55pm after one stop at Leamington Spa. The Pullmans had very quick turnarounds at both ends of the journey; the unit would have reached at Snow Hill at 12.05pm on the 10.10am from London, with one stop at Leamington Spa. It would have left Wolverhampton that morning at 7.00am calling at Snow Hill, Solihull and Leamington, arriving in London at 9.30am. The 1.00pm train usually left from Platform 5, where it had arrived from Paddington, since it could be driven equally well from either end as with modern day Inter-City 125 and other fixed formation sets, so possibly the platform was needed for another train on this day.

Motor Brake Second No. W60096 at the head of the 'Birmingham Pullman' in 1962 after arrival at Platform 5.

Diesels

Lion was the result of a project to build a design which matched the BR Type 4 diesel specification and was undertaken by a consortium made up of the Birmingham Railway Carriage & Wagon Company (BRC&W), Associated Electrical Industries (AEI) and engine manufacturer Sulzer Brothers, which provided its new 2,750bhp 12LDA28-C engine. The external styling followed the principles laid down by the BR Design Panel and their design consultants, Wilkes & Ashmore, and the locomotive was finished in a less than practical but extremely striking white livery, with five gold bands along the lower half of each bodyside, gold cab numbers, and a nameplate incorporating the names of the three consortium members. *Lion* was built at BRC&W's Smethwick Works during 1961 and was completed in April 1962. This photograph of *Lion*, with a BRC&W engineer hanging out of the rear window, was taken during the week commencing 14th May, when No. D0260 began operating a four leg diagram starting with the 7.25am from Wolverhampton to Paddington, returning as far as Wolverhampton on the 12.10pm Paddington to Birkenhead. It then took the 3.35pm back to Paddington and completed its day with the 7.10pm Paddington to Shrewsbury as far as Wolverhampton. The train is about to enter the tunnels at the south end, so this will be either the first (morning) or third (afternoon) leg of the diagram. On 17th May, the locomotive suffered a severe traction motor flashover near Leamington on the fourth leg – ironically this was the first day of crew training on the 'Westerns'. Unfortunately, the consortium 'missed the boat' as far as British Railways was concerned, because the first twenty Brush Type '4's were under construction by the time it appeared and after a short working life of just eighteen months it was withdrawn and scrapped. (Brian Penney)

A new 'Western' diesel-hydraulic, No. D1004 *Western Crusader*, and King No. 6014 *King Henry VII* await departure from Snow Hill on 17th May 1962 with the 1.10 pm Paddington to Birkenhead. No. D1004, which was the last 'Western' turned out from Swindon Works in green livery, was on a positioning move and was attached at Paddington ahead of the 'King' to work as far as Wolverhampton. It was to be used for crew training at Oxley shed starting the following day, along with No. D1000, both being temporarily allocated to Oxley for this purpose. The man standing near the rear cab of No. D1004, hands on hips and in a light coloured pullover is the Old Oak Common Traction Inspector. The locomotive is in the charge of an Old Oak crew; note the second man is wearing a beret. (Brian Penney)

The first 'Western' Class diesel-hydraulic, No. D1000 *Western Enterprise*, waits with the 9.10am Paddington to Birkenhead, a train which the WTT described as running to a 'Special Timing', with a journey time to Snow Hill of exactly two hours. Its experimental desert sand livery is looking in need of a repaint. It did not have a yellow warning panel until November 1962 and was eventually repainted into the standard maroon adopted for the 'Westerns', in October 1964. Unlike the rest of the class, which had a circular carriage style BR roundel, No. D1000 had two cast aluminium BR LMR AC electric pattern crests, which lasted until it was repainted blue in June 1967. Its nameplates were also non-standard and were deeper, the same depth as the numberplates.

Although the 'Peaks' were 'ten-a-penny' at New Street, they were not common at Snow Hill. The June 1963 *The Railway Magazine* reported that 'D123 is currently crew training on local services to Lapworth and Solihull with a view to replacing the Westerns'. Here it is displaying a headcode of 2H55, signifying an ordinary passenger train to the Birmingham Division. It seems that this was a short-lived trial before Brush 'Type 4's were subsequently chosen and crew training on the latter started in November 1963. No. D123 became No. 45125 under the TOPS renumbering in 1974.

The 'Western' hydraulics were replaced on the Paddington-West Midlands services with Brush Type '4's by early 1964. No. D1712 departs northwards past the North Signal Box relay house. Whereas the design of the original North cabin which it replaced had looked very precarious, standing on a single row of columns with the cabin cantilevered on either side, the replacement took the more conventional route of having two sets of columns either side of the track supporting the building above.

Railtour Specials

Preserved 'Pannier' No. 6435 joined with '4F' No. 44188 from Bescot shed on 24th April 1965, to work a Stephenson Locomotive Society tour to mark the closure of the Stratford-upon-Avon & Midland Junction Railway. The pair took the train to Stratford-upon-Avon (GW), and then No. 6435 went solo to Racecourse Junction, handing over there to No. 44188 which ran through Stratford Old Town (S&MJR) and then via Kineton and Fenny Compton to Woodford Halse. They then followed the same itinerary in reverse back to Snow Hill.

Southern Region 'Battle of Britain' 4-6-2 No. 34051 *Winston Churchill* on 23rd May 1965, working an SLS (Midland Area) special, 'The Bulleid 'Pacific' Rail Tour'. The unrebuilt 'Pacific', which was subsequently preserved as part of the National Collection, took the first leg of the tour from Snow Hill to Salisbury, where it handed over to 'Merchant Navy' No. 35017 *Belgian Marine* which took the train to Westbury. The special was returned to Birmingham by No. 7029 *Clun Castle*, arriving at Snow Hill thirteen hours after it had left.

Decline and fall

Snow Hill's decline was rapid following the withdrawal of the London through service in March 1967 and it soon became the largest unstaffed halt in the country. Trains from Stourbridge were diverted to New Street and those from Leamington and Stratford to Moor Street; the tunnel at the south end was closed in March 1968. A lonely single unit diesel car waits at Platform 4 on the ever-decreasing service to Wolverhampton Low Level, as commuters stroll along Platform 5 to the DMU waiting there.

The final public passenger working, the 17.48 to Wolverhampton Low Level, leaves Platform 4 amidst drizzle and before a glum audience on 4th March 1972. Little did anyone in the crowd think that trains would return to Snow Hill fifteen years later. (Robert Darlaston)

10 – Birmingham to Wolverhampton and the Black Country – Western Region

The Great Western Railway main line from Birmingham to Wolverhampton, Shrewsbury and the north west opened between Snow Hill and Wolverhampton Low Level in 1854. It ran through the north eastern part of the 'Black Country' and had intermediate stations at Hockley, Soho & Winson Green, Handsworth & Smethwick, West Bromwich, Swan Village, Wednesbury, Bilston and Priestfield.

The GWR eventually ended up with a monopoly on the south western side of the Black Country but the history of these lines was somewhat more convoluted. The Oxford, Worcester & Wolverhampton Railway (OW&WR) was authorised in 1845 to build a line from the Oxford & Rugby Railway at Wolvercot Junction to Worcester, Stourbridge, Dudley, and Wolverhampton, with a branch to the Grand Junction Railway at Bushbury. The Great Western was closely involved with the project from the start, having a 999 year lease of the line and Isambard Kingdom Brunel was its engineer. There was a considerable row before Parliament passed the Act authorising its construction, mainly about the provision in it that said '*it shall be formed of such a gauge*

... as will admit [it] *being worked continuously with the said Great Western Railway*'. This debate led to the formation of a Royal Commission to investigate the future of railway gauges, which resulted in the Regulation of Gauges Act of 1846 that prescribed 4ft 8½ ins as the standard gauge in Britain, effectively blocking any further broad gauge lines. Ironically, the OW&WR itself was built to the broad gauge but never ran a broad gauge train service.

Construction was beset by further legal problems and inevitably the OW&WR ran out of money, so the GWR was ordered in 1850 to complete the line. Even then, things did not run smoothly, culminating in a riot at Mickleton, near Honeybourne, in a dispute over payment to a contractor. The line to Wolverhampton eventually opened in 1854 and the OW&WR was absorbed into the West Midland Railway in 1860, which itself was absorbed into the GWR in 1863. In the same year, the first part of the Stourbridge Extension was opened, linking Stourbridge with Lye, Cradley Heath and Old Hill, and then to Smethwick and junctions with the L&NWR at Galton Junction and the GWR at Handsworth Junction by 1867.

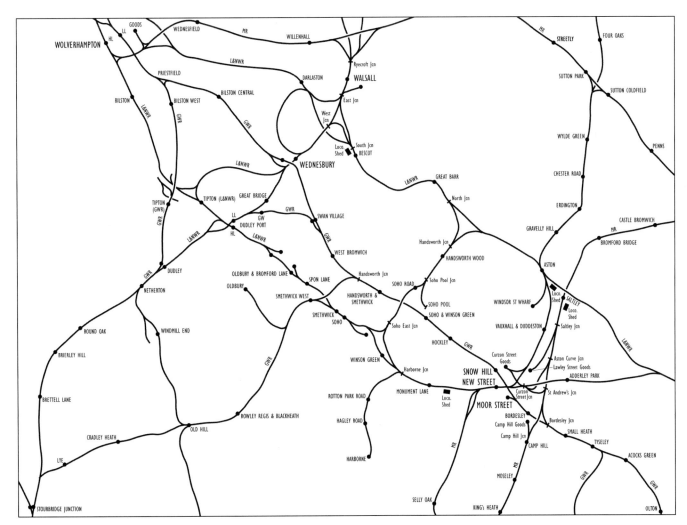

Hockley

Hockley was the primary GWR parcels depot servicing the Birmingham area. Its size was such that, at its peacetime peak, it employed over 1,000 people, utilised 500 road vehicles and handled over half a million tons of parcels and 'smalls' traffic per year. Such was the traffic that, immediately prior to World War Two, three '57xx' pilots were required daily to shunt the yard and thirty-one timetabled trains were dealt with. The service was not interrupted by a direct hit to the extensive offices suffered in 1940, the blast of which blew the roof off the newly completed 'Top Shed', which was the primary transfer building following the re-structure of the three sheds in 1938-40. Like so much of the ex-GWR system in the West Midlands, run-down came in the mid-1960s with final closure in 1967, staff and services being transferred to the LMR depot at Lawley Street.

This view is from a DMU approaching Hockley in the 1960s. The station was unusual in not having a platform on the Down main line, Down trains having to use the relief line if calling at Hockley. A '56xx' 0-6-2T is shunting the yard, with the 1940-built 'Top Shed', the primary parcels depot for the Western Region in Birmingham, visible on the left.

No. 6861 *Crynant Grange* and a '9F' 2-10-0 running light through Hockley in 1963. The 'Grange' was allocated to Tyseley from December 1955 until withdrawn in late 1965 and still has the smaller 3,500 gallon tender. Note the war damage to the former 'Inwards' shed, now termed the 'Bottom Shed' and at this date used for storage.

Stanier 'Coronation' No. 46245 *City of London* from Camden shed passes northbound through Hockley on 29th September 1963, with headcode 0X91 on the smokebox. The carriage window ventilators are open, despite the rain, and the heads sticking out from the door windows identify it as an enthusiasts' special. It was organised by the Warwickshire Railway Society and ran from Birmingham Snow Hill to Crewe (for a visit to the works and sheds) via Wellington and Market Drayton returning via Shrewsbury.

Pontypool Road 'Grange' No. 6819 *Highnam Grange* on a southbound freight at Hockley in 1963. The train was probably the 4V80 5.00am Carlisle-Banbury, which passed through Hockley about 2.35pm and was booked to be hauled by a 'Grange'. The premises of Tearnes & Sons, the transfer manufacturers who made the armorial devices for most railway companies, are in the background. There seemed to be a regular traffic of agricultural equipment on 'Conflat' fitted flat wagons at this period, often appearing as the leading vehicles of southbound freight trains.

Tyseley 'Pannier' No. 9753 at 3.16pm on Saturday 4th October 1958 passing Hockley on an Up freight; this would be the 2.55pm trip from Swan Village to Bordesley Yard, with what was primarily coal empties from Swan Village Gas Works. Note that several of the mineral wagons are still pre-war wooden designs, soon to be displaced by BR standard steel 16-tonners. (Michael Mensing)

Soho & Winson Green

An Old Oak Common 'Castle', probably No. 5093 *Upton Castle*, approaching Soho & Winson Green on the 10.10 am Paddington-Aberystwyth and Pwllheli 'Cambrian Coast Express'. The 'Castle' would take the train as far as Shrewsbury where, at this date, it would hand-over to a 'Manor' which worked through to Aberystwyth, with the Pwllheli portion removed at Machynlleth and probably taken forward by a 'Dukedog' 4-4-0.

The Birmingham Railway Carriage & Wagon Company

The business began as the Birmingham Wagon Company in 1854, financing collieries and merchants wagons before quickly expanding into wagon construction. In 1876, it built its first passenger coaches, with much of the output going to export markets. The name was changed to the Birmingham Railway Carriage & Wagon Company in 1878 and the company began building underground railway stock in 1903, diversifying further into bus bodies for Birmingham Corporation in the 1930s. Its first diesel railcars were produced in 1947 for a railway in Argentina and were soon followed by electric multiple units for Brazil and South Africa, whilst the first diesel locomotives, which went to Australia, appeared in 1954. In the home market, over 600 Mark 1 coaches were delivered to British Railways between 1953 and 1961 and 302 diesel multiple units. Several types of electric multiple units were also produced in conjunction with Metro-Cammell.

BRC&W built 239 main line Type '2' and '3' diesel-electrics and twenty-five AC electric locomotives for British Railways in the late 1950s and early 1960s. Its attempt to gain orders for Type '4' diesels saw the company develop the *Lion* prototype, which was completed in early 1962 but to

no avail. Once the final Type '2' and '3' diesels were completed, there were no more orders from British Railways and with export orders drying-up too, the company took the decision in early 1963 to cease the manufacture of locomotives and rolling stock and to close the Smethwick Works. The factory was rented out and the company, intriguingly renamed the Birmingham Wagon Company, became a property development and financial investment business.

Four of the 1,550hp Type '3' diesel-electrics built by BRC&W for the Southern Region under construction in the shops at Smethwick, probably in early 1962. The last dozen locomotives in the class were built with 7ins narrower bodies for use on the gauge restricted Hastings line and the final one, No. D6597, was completed in May 1962.

Three heads are better than one as No. D0260 *Lion* receives some final adjustments at BRC&W's Smethwick Works on Good Friday, 20th April 1962. The board in front reads 'PROTOTYPE TYPE 4 2750HP DIESEL ELECTRIC LOCOMOTIVE – CO-CO WHEEL ARRANGEMENT. Designed and built by THE BIRMINGHAM RLY CARRIAGE & WAGON CO LTD & FITTED WITH SULZER 12LDA28C DIESEL ENGINE AND ASSOCIATED ELECTRICAL INDUSTRIES TRACTION & CONTROL EQUIPMENT'. The new Type '2' just visible on the right is probably the short-lived No. D5383, which was released into traffic a few days after this picture was taken. This was the unfortunate locomotive written-off after a collision in August 1965 at East Langton, while working a Leicester-Wellingborough freight.

Lion in pristine white on test north of Handsworth station in April 1962, probably on one of its first outings. During its early workings, *Lion* could always be observed with pristine white buffers. This was because it was driven from the 'A' end only and was turned at Stafford Road and Ranelagh Bridge, Paddington after each trip.

Handsworth & Smethwick West

No. D1036 *Western Emperor* passing Handsworth & Smethwick station with the Royal Train on 24th May 1963, the very first time a 'Western' hauled the monarch in the West Midlands district. It had left Paddington the previous day for Kings Sutton station near Banbury, and had been stabled overnight at Adderbury, which by this date was the terminus of the line which had originally run through to Kingham. No. D1036 remained attached to the train while steam heating was provided overnight by two specially prepared 'Manors'. The Queen was visiting Birmingham city centre to view work on the redevelopment of the Bull Ring Shopping Centre and to open a section of the Inner Ring Road. On this day, she had left the train at Birmingham and would rejoin it at Wolverhampton Low Level, where it would revert to 1X01, the code 1X00 being used when she was not on the train but her staff were still aboard. Western Emperor was the second of the Crewe-built locomotives, entering service in August 1962 and one of only three 'Westerns' never to carry maroon livery – it went straight from green into blue in November 1966. No. D1036 was unique because, from new, its numberplates were positioned higher, almost level with the cab door handle rather than in line with the nameplates. The sidings on the right lead to the Birmingham Railway Carriage & Wagon Company factory, the birthplace of the Lion prototype and over two hundred Type '2' and Type '3' diesels. Behind the photographer, the four lines became two where the line to Stourbridge Junction branched off at Handsworth Junction.

A post-war Stanier Class '5' from Edge Hill shed, No. 44772 on a fitted freight in about 1964 at Handsworth & Smethwick. Its upper lamp bracket has been moved down onto the smokebox door away from live overhead wires for safety reasons but note that the centre bracket has also been moved to the right, so it is still underneath the upper one.

BR Standard '5MT' No. 73020 approaching Handsworth & Smethwick in 1967 on the Down main. It had been transferred to Guildford shed in March 1967 and would be withdrawn in July when the Southern Region eliminated steam. The chalked headcode on the smokebox is 1V32, so the train is probably from either Eastbourne or Margate to Wolverhampton. This would be a Saturday working and the locomotive would remain at Oxley before returning the following Saturday. Oxley would use the Southern Standard 'Class 5' during the week for local services much to the joy of the local spotters. The Southern shed would do the same with the Oxley Class '5' that it received in the other direction.

Class '5101' No. 4105 on Sunday 25th September 1960 passing Smethwick West at 11.59am. There was no booked train around this time on a Sunday, so it is probably a Stourbridge Junction-Bordesley special. No. 4105 had just been transferred to Tyseley from Exeter. The passengers on the left, including several anglers, were waiting for the arrival of the 11.50am Birmingham Snow Hill to Cardiff train. The station had been renamed in 1956 from Smethwick Junction. (Michael Mensing)

West Bromwich and The Hawthorns

Tyseley-based '57xx' 0-6-0PT No. 9753 east of West Bromwich station on an Up freight on Saturday 30th September 1958. Note that the 16-ton mineral wagons are sheeted over to protect their loads. (Michael Mensing)

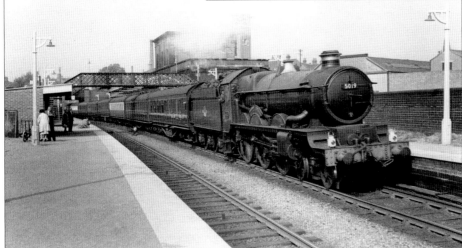

No. 5019 *Treago Castle* passing through West Bromwich on the 7.20am Pwllheli-Paddington on Saturday 13th September 1958. The 'Castle' had been transferred to Wolverhampton Stafford Road the previous May. (Michael Mensing)

No. 6020 *King Henry IV* roars through West Bromwich on Saturday 20th September 1958 with the 7.30am Shrewsbury-Paddington. (Michael Mensing)

No. 2885 runs through West Bromwich on an Up freight at 12.41pm on 17th September 1958. It must be a special coal empties as no Class 'H' freight was booked at that time. Built in 1938, No. 2885 was the second of the updated 2-8-0s with side window cab and outside steampipes, and was allocated to Tyseley for less than a year, from June 1958 until April 1959. (Michael Mensing)

Class '43xx' 2-6-0 No. 7315 from Worcester shed taking the Stourbridge line at Handsworth Junction and passing The Hawthorns Halt on Saturday 16th September 1961. This had been opened on Christmas Day 1931 for the use of football supporters travelling to the nearby West Bromwich Albion Football Club's ground 'The Hawthorns' and was only open on match days. The floodlights of the football stadium are visible in the background. One of the rudimentary wooden platform shelters had been moved to here from Dolserau Halt near Dolgellau which closed in 1951. It still bore the name Dolserau but there is no evidence of any passenger alighting in error! The halt closed in March 1968 but a new station was built there in 1999 when the Midland Metro line was opened. (Michael Mensing)

Wednesbury

These pictures taken at Wednesbury in the 1950s and early 1960s show the Great Western line from Birmingham to Wolverhampton against a background of what is best described as an industrial wasteland. The dereliction is already setting in, although the rows of terraced houses are still occupied and the factories are still working.

A '41xx' with a local going towards Birmingham at Wednesbury in the 1950s, about to cross over the Birmingham Canal Navigation Tame (or Teme) Valley Branch. In the left background are the factories of Walsh Graham, now an industrial estate, and Charles (Wednesbury) Ltd who produced washers by the million, of all types in both steel and brass. The L&NWR South Staffordshire line from Walsall to Dudley crossed underneath just beyond the left edge of the picture.

'Castle' No. 5055 *Earl of Eldon* emerges from the 412 yards long Hill Top Tunnel with a northbound express. It is running downhill on a 1 in 97 the gradient, which provided a stiff challenge to trains going the other way towards Birmingham, although the gradient reduced slightly to 1 in 147 inside the tunnel. The tunnel's broad gauge origins are clear to see.

A later pattern 2-8-0, '2884' Class No. 3809, slogging up the 1 in 97 towards Hill Top Tunnel with an Up freight in the late 1950s. It was allocated to Cardiff Canton until the end of 1960. The first wagon in the train is an ex-GWR 'Mica' van which is painted white underneath the grime.

One of the earlier '28xx' 2-8-0s, No. 2854, coasts down the bank from Hill Top Tunnel in the 1950s with a coal train. It was at Oxley from late 1949 until March 1956, when it was transferred to Shrewsbury, although it only stayed there for a month before moving on again to Gloucester Horton Road.

Class '94xx' 0-6-0PT No. 9496 on an Up trip working of coal empties. It was built by the Yorkshire Engine Company in 1954 and was at Stafford Road for the mere five years it was in service. It was probably on the No. 33 Bank trip, which went to Priestfield, Wednesbury and Swan Village.

Oxley-based '57xx' No. 9768 with loaded coal wagons on a trip freight.

Another '28xx' 2-8-0, No. 2849, blasts its way up the incline out of Wednesbury. The 1912-built engine was shedded at Tyseley until the end of 1959. The leading bogie bolster is carrying three large girders which overlap the wagon, so an empty plate wagon acts as a 'runner'. It would be interesting to know the weight of the load!

Class '43xx' No. 5370 is working hard up the 1 in 97 with a long unfitted freight. The Churchward 2-6-0 was allocated to Oxley until late 1959.

'Modified Hall' No. 7918 *Rhose Wood Hall* leaves an impressive smoke trail as it climbs up towards Hill Top Tunnel, probably in 1962. It was at Tyseley from new in 1950 until withdrawn in 1965.

One of the first batch of 'Halls' built by the Great Western Railway in 1929, No. 4908 *Broome Hall*, with a Down relief during the time it was shedded at Oxford, between November 1961 and August 1962. The train reporting board has slipped to one side and the crew have abandoned it, chalking '1V' and the number onto the smokebox door. The first coach is of Southern Railway origin, having almost flat sides to conform with the Hastings Line loading gauge.

Well turned out No. 6025 *King Henry III* with a Down express in 1962. This was the last year that the 'Kings' would rule on the West Midlands expresses, 'Western' diesels took over from 10th September and all of the class were withdrawn by the end of the year.

No. 1002 *County of Berks* showing its mixed traffic credentials on an Up express freight. The Hawksworth 'County' was at Shrewsbury from November 1962 until withdrawn in September 1963.

No. 1019 *County of Merioneth* on the Up 'Pines Express' from Manchester to Bournemouth. From September 1962, the 'Pines' had been re-routed via Shrewsbury, Wellington and Wolverhampton and then south from here via Oxford, Reading and Basingstoke to Southampton, taking it away from the Somerset & Dorset Joint line. It was the 'Pines' running over the S&D part of the route which had seen it achieve a level of fame some way above its importance in comparison to other similar named trains. English Electric Type '4's brought the train to Wolverhampton and normally handed over to a Stafford Road 'Castle', which took it as far as Oxford. No. 1019 was at Shrewsbury from October 1962 until withdrawn in February 1963.

No. 4094 *Dynevor Castle*, with steam leaking, ascends the incline to Hill Top in the late 1950s. The 'Castle' was shedded at Wolverhampton Stafford Road until June 1957.

No. 4955 *Plaspower Hall* under easy steam as it runs down the gradient from Hill Top in the mid-1950s. The first coach is a post-war GWR design and the second a former GWR 'Cornish Riviera Express' Centenary stock saloon.

No. 5022 *Wigmore Castle* on a Wolverhampton to Paddington express in the early 1960s. A Stafford Road engine from 1948 until withdrawn in 1963, it was fitted with a double chimney in February 1959.

Stafford Road 'Castle' No. 5031 *Totnes Castle* before it was fitted with a double chimney during a Heavy General overhaul from 24th April until 24th June 1959.

No. 5034 *Corfe Castle* from Old Oak Common had been fitted with a double chimney during a Heavy Intermediate overhaul at Swindon between December 1960 and February 1961.

Large 'Prairie' No. 6139 appears to have taken over a Down express from a failed passenger engine judging by the stock with its headboards. It still has its local passenger headlamp which reinforces the case that it was an emergency substitute. This was one of the six '61xx' Class engines transferred to Tyseley in 1953 to replace BR Standard '82xxx' Class 3 2-6-2Ts sent to South Wales.

No. 6996 *Blackwell Hall* on an Up passenger train in the mid-1950s has Class '3' fitted freight headlamps. Underneath the grime it still appears to be in lined black livery, which suggests the picture may have been taken while it was shedded at Old Oak Common between May 1952 and August 1954, although it seems more likely to be after that date when it had moved to Taunton.

No. 7012 *Barry Castle* from Old Oak Common on a Down express in 1962. It has just passed under the bridge which carried the long closed Balls Hill Branch Canal immediately after the northbound exit from Hill Top Tunnel.

No. 7905 *Fowey Hall*, piloting a 'Castle' in the 1960s, was at Banbury from November 1959 until withdrawn in May 1964. The first four coaches are Bulleid stock, which had a slightly different profile to the BR Mark 1 coaches that were very similar in design.

'Modified Hall' No. 6971 *Athelhampton Hall* with an excursion on the Down line at Wednesbury just north of the station. The large building in the background is the Patent Shaft Steel Works Ltd's Monway Works. The line in the foreground leads to the Willingsworth Iron Co. Works, which was a subsidiary of the Patent Shaft company that had closed by 1961; the line was used to access the Wagon Repairs Ltd wagon works. Patent Shaft itself closed in 1980 after nearly 150 years in operation. Its origins, as the name suggests, were in the manufacture of a patented iron axle, the business expanding in the late 19th century to produce wheels, tyres and other products for railways, as well as producing the world's first steel bridges.

Two 'Pannier' tanks on what is most likely the 8T76 1.00pm empties from Swan Village Gas Works to Wednesbury. No. 3782 had been transferred to Oxley in August 1964 and No. 3744 in January 1965. The flat bottom track in the foreground is on a shunting neck while the main line was still bullhead.

These Derby built high-density three car units, later Class '116', were little different from the steam stock they replaced in June 1957, when DMUs took over most of the suburban services from Birmingham Snow Hill. The seating was cramped, whilst the slam doors to each bay and the droplight windows were draughty. They were painted in drab unlined Brunswick green, relieved only by yellow 'speed whiskers' and the white fibreglass cab roof. This unit was on a Snow Hill to Wellington service.

There is no sign of life on the platforms of Wednesbury Central, the ex-Great Western station, looking north on 4th July 1964. The signalman has parked his scooter in front of Wednesbury South Box on the Up platform. Wednesbury was almost identical to the other station buildings at Bilston, West Bromwich and Handsworth & Smethwick which were built by the Birmingham, Wolverhampton & Dudley Railway in 1854. Wednesbury Central, together with West Bromwich and Banbury stations, had lamp posts of Southern Region design, perhaps an early example of inter-regional co-operation. (Robert Darlaston)

Dudley

The arrangement of the two stations at Dudley was rather curious. The GWR station was on the line to Wolverhampton and the L&NWR station was on that company's line to Walsall. The junction between the lines was to the south, towards Stourbridge. L&NWR passenger trains from Walsall reversed in their station and had no contact with the Great Western but the GWR trains from Snow Hill ran over L&NWR metals from Great Bridge Junction and also terminated in the L&NWR station. The GWR station was used by Old Hill trains, Stourbridge to Wolverhampton trains and by a handful of Stourbridge Junction to Snow Hill trains which ran via Brettell Lane and Dudley: after calling at the GWR station they reversed back towards Stourbridge until clear of the junction and then continued non-stop through the L&NWR station en route to Snow Hill.

Class '64xx' No. 6434 spent much of its life in South Wales and was transferred from Tondu to Stourbridge shed in October 1963, from where it was withdrawn in September 1964. This picture at Dudley shows it with an auto-train which, having arrived from Old Hill into the Down platform, has moved forward and is now backing into the Down Sidings. The driver is still in the driving compartment of the coach and is indicating to the fireman, who is driving the train, when the back end is clear of the points.

Gloucester Railway Carriage & Wagon Company single unit No. W55018 and two coaches of a three-car suburban DMU, later Class '116', make up a service train at Dudley on Sunday 14th June 1964, with the 8.10pm to Birmingham Snow Hill, the last train on the last day of this service. (Michael Mensing)

Bilston

No. 6954 *Lotherton Hall* at Bilston on a South Coast-Birkenhead express in around 1952. The 'Hall' was allocated to Bristol St. Philips Marsh shed from August 1951.

No. 4106, probably on the same date as No. 6954 above, at Bilston with a Birmingham-Wolverhampton four coach local. This '5101' Class 2-6-2T was transferred to Landore, South Wales, in October 1952.

Wolverhampton Low Level

The two stations at Wolverhampton were literally feet apart in both the vertical and horizontal directions but operated entirely separately for over a century. Low Level was rebuilt in 1869 but little changed after that date until 1967, when the through London trains finished and the tracks at the north end were lifted. It became a terminus with just the dying embers of the local DMU service from Birmingham Snow Hill until that ceased in 1972 but even then lingered on as a parcels depot.

Two spotters chat with the crew as they admire 'King' No. 6018 *King Henry VI* in August 1962, after its arrival at Wolverhampton Low Level from Paddington with the original 'Inter-City' which had been introduced in September 1950. It is interesting that the name went on to be used by British Rail to describe all of its principal express services and was even adopted by German Railways (who still use the title). The last normal revenue-earning trip by a 'King' is believed to have been by No. 6011 *King James I*, with reliefs to the Down and Up 'Cambrian Coast Express' on 21st December 1962, the 10.50am Paddington to Shrewsbury and return. No 6018 was returned to service in 1963, after the class had all been withdrawn at the end of 1962, to work the Stephenson Locomotive Society's 'Farewell to the Kings Tour' on 28th April 1963 from Birmingham to Swindon and back.

No. 7024 *Powis Castle* departing with an Up express in August 1962. It was transferred from Old Oak Common to Stafford Road in August 1961 and then to Oxley in September 1963, before withdrawal in 1965. The condition of the leading Hawksworth coach leaves a lot to be desired. Through trains from Birkenhead usually had an engine change and were strengthened with additional coaches and a Restaurant Car at Wolverhampton, with the opposite procedure taking place in the Down direction.

'Modified Hall' No. 6963 *Throwley Hall* clanks through with a Down Class '7' freight. It was allocated to 81D Reading for just over six months in late 1964. The station is almost deserted apart from a couple of railwaymen, two spotters (one with his Mum!) and the ever present parcels barrows.

Class '57xx' 0-6-0PT No. 9776 working as Wolverhampton Low Level pilot on 2nd March 1965. It had moved up from Merthyr Tydfil to Oxley in May 1964, after many years at various Welsh sheds. The cabside number plate has disappeared to be replaced by a well executed hand-painted version. No. 9776 was withdrawn in April 1966. Note the fire irons are correctly stowed on the bunker hooks.

No. 6934 *Beachamwell Hall* in 1964 with a northbound parcels train. The engine had been transferred from Shrewsbury to Banbury in October and was withdrawn a year later. Its original Collett tender with flared top has been replaced by a Hawksworth flat sided tender.

Oxley

Oxley shed in Wolverhampton was opened in 1907, as a satellite of nearby Stafford Road which by then had reached capacity. It had two standard Great Western twenty-eight road roundhouses, arranged end to end rather than the more usual side by side configuration because of the space constraints of the location. It was sited immediately opposite to Oxley Sidings and hence housed mainly freight engines, the passenger locomotives being

dealt with at Stafford Road. It was one of the last strongholds of Great Western steam with one '57xx' "Pannier" surviving until late 1966 in an allocation consisting almost entirely of ex-LM&SR types. The shed itself was closed in March 1967 but a new facility on the site is still used for 'Pendolino' trains. The route between Wolverhampton High Level and Oxley depot was the first part of the former Great Western Railway to be electrified at 25KV.

Churchward '47xx' No. 4704 from Old Oak Common in one of the roundhouses at Oxley on 29th April 1962. The big 2-8-0s spent their life working express freights, mostly overnight, from London to Plymouth and the West Midlands, and No. 4704 would have been a regular visitor to the shed.

One of the later '28xx' 2-8-0s with Collett side-window cab, No. 3802, on 18th February 1962 alongside No. 6851 Hurst Grange. No. 3802 had been at Oxley since May 1952 but moved to Tyseley in October 1962.

On 18th February 1962, BR Standard '3MT' 2-6-2T No. 82041 looks immaculate in the lined green which Swindon managed to apply to many of the Western Region passenger tank engines in the late 1950s, instead of the black in which they were previously painted. It was built at Swindon in June 1955 and had the same Swindon No. 4 boiler as the GWR '5101' and '56xx' classes. At the date of this picture, it was allocated to Bath Green Park on the Somerset & Dorset Joint line and so may have been running-in after repair at Stafford Road Works. Although officially withdrawn in December 1965, No. 82041 was observed on a Bath Green Park to Bristol service on 1st January 1966.

The tender on '2251' 0-6-0 No. 3200 dwarfs the engine in one of the Oxley roundhouses on 18th February 1962. No. 3200 was shedded at Oswestry at this date but was transferred to the Somerset & Dorset Joint shed at Templecombe in December 1963. It is also likely to have had attention at Stafford Road Works.

No. 5953 *Dunley Hall* from Bristol St. Philips Marsh on 18th February 1962, would be withdrawn in October 1962. Just above the smokebox of the 'Hall' can be seen the flip-down plate onto which loaded loco coal tubs were manually pushed and tipped. The self-propelled crane would be fitted with a grab bucket and usually used to clear ash and clinker, as opposed to coaling engines.

'Crab' No. 42936 and a Stanier 2-6-0 demonstrate that the London Midland takeover of the former Great Western lines in the Midlands was well underway. No. 42936 had been transferred to Birkenhead Mollington Street from Longsight in November 1960 and was withdrawn from there in July 1965. *The Railway Observer* of January 1962 reported that 'through workings of LMR engines to Oxley and other Western Region Midlands depots are increasing'. After the depot was taken over by the LMR in January 1963, the ex-Great Western classes lingered on for another couple of years, with '57xx' "Pannier"'s and 'Granges' fighting the rearguard action but all had gone by October 1966, replaced by diesel shunters, and Stanier '8F's and Class '5's.

Oxley was very much a steam shed, so although D1011 *Western Thunderer* is outside the lifting shop, it is highly unlikely that any diesel locomotive was ever lifted there. Though the lifting shop was only for the use of steam locomotives it was, comparatively speaking, the cleanest part of the depot and therefore was regularly used to house diesel locomotives. Servicing would have been at the more basic level of the 'A' or 'B' examination equivalent of much later years – fuel, coolant and engine room checks, etc. More involved work would have been carried out at Old Oak Common or Laira, which, from 10th September 1962, received locomotives off the triangular diagrams which included the route 'to the north'.

Stafford Road shed

The shed was built in 1854 by the Great Western Railway on the opposite side of the Stafford Road to the Shrewsbury & Birmingham Railway works, near to Wolverhampton Low Level station. It was expanded in a piecemeal fashion during the late 19th century, the old broad gauge sheds lasting until the 1930s, when there was a major rebuilding using cheap government money provided under the Development (Loan Guarantees & Grants) Act, 1929. Two new steel-framed sheds, a lifting and erection shop, and coaling stage were built. Stafford Road, with its 'Kings' and 'Castles', shared the express passenger work on the Paddington-Birmingham-Chester route with Old Oak Common, the freight duties having been taken over by its satellite shed at Oxley in the early 1900s. The elimination of steam on the London to West Midlands expresses in September 1962 and the takeover of the Western Region lines in the Midlands by the LMR in January 1963 made closure inevitable and the run-down shed was closed in September 1963.

Two Old Oak Common engines, No. 5082 *Powis Castle* and 'Modified Hall' No. 6978 *Haroldstone Hall*, outside Stafford Road shed on 19th March 1961.

No. 6001 *King Edward VII* on 19th March 1961 at its home shed of Wolverhampton Stafford Road. It was allocated there from late 1954 until withdrawn in September 1962. The 'King' is preparing to move off shed to work train the 'A91' train number, more correctly 1A91, the 3.35pm from Wolverhampton to Paddington.

No. 1016 *County of Hants* on 18th February 1962. It was grammatically correct to use abbreviated titles such as Hants, Bucks, Chester, etc, as 'County of Hampshire' would be incorrect – a lesson that was learned on the earlier GWR Churchward 'County' 4-4-0s. No. 1016 was shedded at Shrewsbury from November 1952 until withdrawn in September 1963.

Another long-time Shrewsbury 'County' No. 1025 *County of Radnor* in the early 1960s. The box-like appearance of the Hawksworth tenders shows up well. The tenders fitted to the 'Counties' were 6 inches wider than those built with the 'Modified Halls' and so were not interchangeable. The 'Counties' were unique among the GWR named passenger engines in having straight nameplates, that were necessary because of the full-length splasher over the wheels, instead of separate splashers for each wheel over which the standard curved nameplates were fitted.

One of the last class designed by the GWR but not introduced until late 1949, Hawksworth lightweight '16xx' 'Pannier' No. 1661 from Worcester shed was built as late as March 1955. Pictured on 19th March 1961 at Stafford Road shed, it still has the spark-arresting chimney fitted for working on the Cleobury Mortimer & Ditton Priors Light Railway, where the principal traffic of the line was naval ordnance for the Royal Naval Armaments Depot. No. 1661 was transferred to Worcester in 1957, where it regularly worked the short branch to Hill, Evans & Co's Vinegar Works. The clean front end suggests it may have been in Stafford Road Works, though whether the non-standard front numberplate, which looks like a flat sheet of metal with the number simply painted on, was fitted then is unknown.

Collett '14xx' 0-4-2T No. 1451, in smart lined green passenger livery, was almost certainly fresh from Stafford Road Works at this date, since it was not a local engine, being allocated to Exeter shed throughout the late 1950s, before moving to Gloucester Horton Road in November 1963.

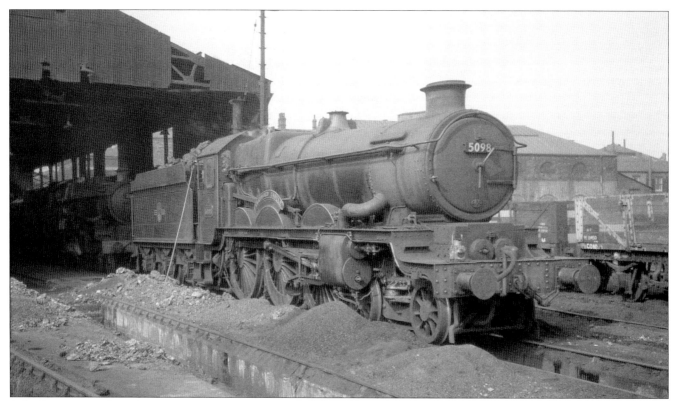

A double chimneyed 'Castle' from Llanelly, No. 5098 *Clifford Castle*, on 7th April 1963. The chimney was fitted at Swindon during a Heavy General repair in late 1958 and No. 5098 was transferred to Old Oak Common the month after this picture was taken, moving to Reading in April 1964 for its last two months before withdrawal.

A forlorn No. 6022 *King Edward III* on 7th April 1963 outside Stafford Road shed. Although withdrawn in the previous September and shorn of its plates, it is otherwise intact and sporting a grubby 'NOT TO BE MOVED' plate on the smokebox door.

Stafford Road Works

Stafford Road Works date back to 1849, when the Shrewsbury & Birmingham Railway began construction of an engine shed and repair shop here. When the Great Western absorbed the S&BR in 1854, it located the headquarters of its Northern Division at Wolverhampton and developed the works to repair the growing number of standard gauge locomotives which were not able to travel to Swindon on the still broad gauge tracks. The works soon began to build new standard gauge engines and a 'Wolverhampton' style emerged. This went on until the early 1900s, by which time the size of the new Churchward designs had

outgrown the layout of the old works. The ten 2-6-2Ts built there had to have their buffers and pony trucks removed in order to get them out of the building and so no more new engines were built after 1908. The works was modernised in the early 1930s under the Government Loans & Guarantees Act, with a new 450 feet long erecting shop, equipped with four 50-ton travelling cranes, opened in 1932. In 1960, the Western Region drew up plans to close the works and convert it to a diesel maintenance and repair shop for the West Midlands but this was not implemented and it closed in June 1964.

Class '4575' 2-6-2T No. 5572, all the way from St Blazey in Cornwall, on 19th March 1961. It was transferred to Plymouth Laira immediately after its overhaul was completed but its stay there was brief because it was withdrawn in April 1962.

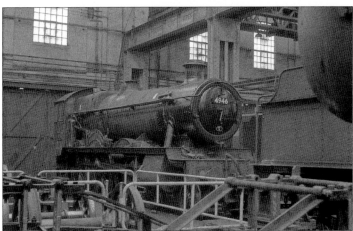

The smokebox of No. 4946 *Moseley Hall* had already been repainted when photographed on 18th February 1962. The 'Hall' was allocated to Shrewsbury from April 1960 until withdrawn in June 1963.

No. 3833 is partly stripped down on 18th February 1962. The Class '2884' 2-8-0 was at Cardiff Canton until withdrawn in July 1963. In front of it is No. 6976 *Graythwaite Hall* from Banbury shed.

No. 5095 *Barbury Castle*, photographed inside the works on 18th February 1962, had recently arrived from Shrewsbury, where it was shedded between April 1960 and withdrawal in August 1962. The extent of any work done on this visit to Stafford Road was probably minimal and is likely to have been a Casual repair, with attention to the inside piston valves; note the interesting assembly attached to the front buffer beam to facilitate valve examination. The double chimney was fitted in November 1958 and the Hawksworth tender in September 1960.

No. 5977 *Beckford Hall* is surrounded by the clutter typical of a steam locomotive works on 18th February 1962. It was from Reading shed, where it was allocated from February 1960 until withdrawn in August 1963.

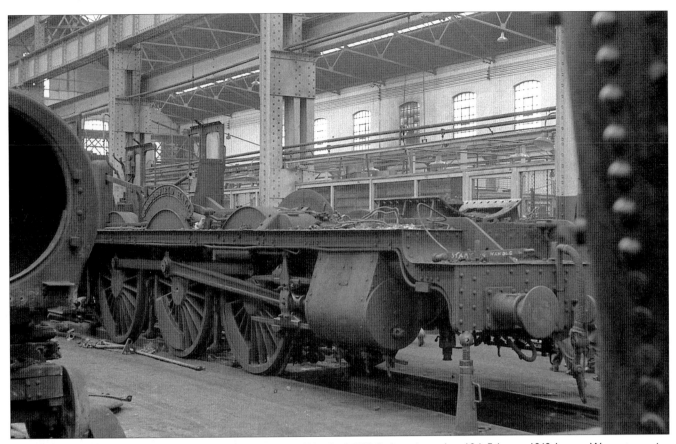

The boiler and smokebox had been lifted off 'Modified Hall' No. 6992 *Arborfield Hall* when pictured on 18th February 1962. It was a Worcester engine from September 1959 until withdrawn in June 1964.

No. 7200, the first GWR 2-8-2T, was converted from '42xx' 2-8-0T No. 5275 in 1934, when the Great Western decided to increase the operational usefulness of the class by increasing their fuel capacity, by two tons of coal and 700 gallons of water, to almost that of a tender engine. The frames were lengthened by over four feet to accommodate the greatly enlarged bunker, which also needed the addition of a rear radial truck. No. 7200, pictured on 18th February 1962, was shedded at Llanelly from November 1960 until withdrawn in July 1963.

Windmill End

Windmill End was a station on the Great Western Railway 'Bumble Hole' line between Netherton and Old Hill. It provided an alternative GWR route from Handsworth to Wolverhampton, avoiding Wednesbury but serving Dudley. Windmill End opened in 1878, was de-staffed in 1952 and, despite being refurbished in the early 1960s, was closed in June 1964, four years before the line itself closed. It was immortalised in 1963 as the closing line

of the song '*Slow Train*' by Michael Flanders and Donald Swann. This comic ditty about the railways which would soon be lost under rationalisation was first performed as part of their 1963 musical revue '*At the Drop of Another Hat*' and it included many other stations that were earmarked for closure in the Beeching Report. By the end of the 1970s, the site of the railway and the station had been obliterated and it is now parkland.

The boy sitting on the bridge parapet is precariously close to the line, as a '5101' 2-6-2T banks a freight for Dudley up the 1 in 53 incline. The train is crossing a bridge over the Dudley Canal Navigations Line No. 2, which connected Dudley with the Worcester & Birmingham Canal.

Churchward 'Star' No. 4061 *Glastonbury Abbey* on a short express heading towards Dudley. The trains shown here and in the following pictures had probably been diverted from the main line through Wednesbury because of engineering work. The 'Bumble Hole' line was often used for such purposes and expresses did not otherwise use the route. *Glastonbury Abbey* was one of the final batch of 'Stars' built in 1922-3 and named after Abbeys. No. 4061 was allocated to Wolverhampton Stafford Road from 1950 onwards and was one of the last two 'Stars' in service when withdrawn in March 1957, outlived only by No. 4056 *Princess Margaret*, which lasted until October of that year. The chimneys in the background belong to Doulton & Co. Ltd, whose pipeworks manufactured drainpipes and conduits, stacks of which can just be glimpsed to the left of No. 4061. Building work is underway to the right.

A bunker-first '5101' 2-6-2T assists an equally unidentified 'Castle' through the Windmill End platforms in the early 1950s.

Class '5101' No. 4140 working back from Netherton in front of a 'Castle' in the mid-1950s. After passing through the station on the short stretch of level track, both locomotives will attack the 1 in 50, easing to 1 in 58, towards Old Hill. The 'Prairie' was allocated to Wolverhampton Stafford Road from late 1954 until January 1958, when it was transferred to Stourbridge Junction.

Brierley Hill

Class '57xx' 0-6-0PT No. 9733 at 7.24pm on the Saturday evening of 26th August 1961, drifting through Brierley Hill with a short southbound freight. It had been transferred from Tyseley to Stourbridge Junction the previous month. (Michael Mensing)

Brettell Lane

No. 8498 at Brettell Lane on the 5.27pm Stourbridge Junction to Wolverhampton Low Level, on Whit Monday 11th June 1962. The Hawksworth designed 'Pannier' was built in November 1952 by Robert Stephenson & Hawthorns Ltd at their Darlington Works and was shedded at Stafford Road when this picture was taken. It was transferred to Old Oak Common in July 1963. The heavy engineering traffic of the area necessitated the substantial fixed position crane seen in the goods yard. (Michael Mensing)

Old Hill

This picture taken at Old Hill in late 1963 or early 1964 shows '64xx' 0-6-0PT No. 6434 with a train that has just arrived from Dudley via the Windmill End 'Bumble Hole' line. To make the return trip to Dudley it will pull forward, and then reverse over a crossover behind the photographer, to pass through the opposite platform. The right hand signal of the bracket in front of the box controlled access to the 'Bumble Hole' line. The freight line to Halesowen is visible in the left background. The photograph is interesting in that it shows that the decline of the old GWR stations had already begun. Only a few years earlier in 1958, a picture taken from the same viewpoint shows substantial buildings and awnings on the opposite platform, which then had a second face for the Halesowen line.

Stourbridge Junction shed's '56xx' Class 0-6-2T No. 6678 climbing through Old Hill with a freight from the Dudley line on Saturday 30th May 1959. (Michael Mensing)

A lone trainspotter watches No. 3819 from Didcot shed on 30th September 1962, climbing into Old Hill tunnel with the northbound Stanlow-Rowley Regis fuel oil train, which was being banked by '5101' 2-6-2T No. 4173 in the rear. The area was riddled with old mine workings with subsidence far from uncommon, hence the props holding up the tunnel mouth. (Michael Mensing)

Lye

In the early 1950s, 'Grange' 4-6-0 No. 6853 *Morehampton Grange*, a long-time resident of Tyseley shed, rolls into Lye station, displaying express headcode lamps and heading for Stourbridge. In the distance is Lye Signal Box, used to control both the once busy sidings whose large goods shed is screened by the train and the junction for the short goods branch to Hayes Lane, which served three brickworks and a colliery until closure in 1964. The footbridge has been partially replaced using pre-cast steps and banisters, the original cast iron and lattice span being retained. On the Up platform a porter waits for the next train, having already positioned his trolley ready for the expected mail. Sundries traffic was a healthy source of revenue for the former GWR lines in the West Midlands and is demonstrated by the tin bath awaiting onward shipment. It is a reminder that the railways were then a 'common carrier', legally required to accept parcels irrespective of size for shipment throughout the country.

Hagley and Stourbridge

Ex-GWR '2251' 0-6-0 No. 2270 near Hagley on Stourbridge Trip No. 7 'Bank Train' in December 1949, the 12.00pm Stourbridge Junction-Elmley Lovett Sidings. The class was a modernised version of the 'Dean Goods', using the same Swindon No. 10 taper boiler as used on the rebuilt Taff Vale 0-6-2Ts and fitted with a side window cab. No. 2270 was built in April 1930 and was withdrawn in September 1959.

A '57xx' 0-6-0PT at Stourbridge Junction heading for Kidderminster with a mixed freight circa 1949. The photograph was taken from the steps to Stourbridge South Signal Box, looking back to the carriage sidings where a 2-6-2T is marshalling a train.

Class '5101' 2-6-2T No. 4115 arriving at Stourbridge Junction on a Birmingham-Worcester local which includes several parcels vehicles. No. 4115 was allocated to Hereford between December 1958 and February 1963, when it was transferred to Severn Tunnel Junction and this picture was taken before the former shed's code was changed from 85C to 86C in January 1961. The Stourbridge Town Branch can be seen diverging on the left.

Auto fitted '64xx' Class 0-6-0PT No. 6422 ready to propel its auto-trailer from Stourbridge Town up the 1 in 67 for the 22 chain journey to Stourbridge Junction in the mid-1950s. The 'Pannier' had been at Wolverhampton Stafford Road shed since October 1946 and remained there until withdrawal in 1962. Note the top left hand advertisement for the Cattle & Poultry Show at Bingley Hall in Birmingham in November. The track on the left is the Stourbridge Goods Branch, which was operated quite separately from the passenger line. The branch was originally double track but in 1935 was 'split' into two parallel lines, one for passenger and one for goods use, both worked on the 'one engine in steam' principle.

Diesel railcar No. W14W at Stourbridge Town in 1957, with a service over the 1,600 yards long branch from Stourbridge Junction. The railcars took over from the previous steam powered auto-train at the end of 1956. In the 1950s, two of these railcars normally operated the complete off-peak Snow Hill to Dudley shuttle between them, all through the day but augmented by steam in the rush hour, as well as shuttling backwards and forwards on the short distance service between Old Hill and Dudley. Note the track looks freshly ballasted.

Stourbridge Town with a DMU from the Junction on 6th August 1966. The goods line on the right was restricted to a maximum of thirty goods wagons, or twenty-five if they carried coal or minerals, because of the severe gradient down from the junction, mostly at 1 in 67. The station received the enamel nameboard Stourbridge Town in 1957, having made do for many years with the original GWR board which omitted the 'Town'. (Robert Darlaston)

Gloucester Railway Carriage & Wagon Company single unit No. W55012 at Stourbridge Town in the early 1970s, in a picture which contrasts sharply with the one above. The goods line has been lifted, the platform canopies and the 'Iron Mink' van body have gone but the chocolate and cream enamel sign is still there. The station was demolished in 1979 to make space for a new bus station but the branch was not closed, a 'bus shelter' and ticket office being built a few yards down the now slightly curtailed line. The branch was again shortened slightly and another new station built in 1994, whilst it has been worked since 2009 by two Class '139' Parry People-mover units, which are powered by stored flywheel energy.

Outside cylindered '1366' Class 0-6-0PT No. 1369 was a long way from its Weymouth home on 18th February 1962. The state of its paintwork indicates it was returning from a Heavy General overhaul at Stafford Road Works, one of only two instances of the class being serviced there. Apparently, Stourbridge held on to the engine for a few weeks and regularly used it on pilot duties and trips to and from Stourbridge Junction goods yard, before finally sending it back to Weymouth. No. 1369 was completed in February 1934 and was a shunter at Swindon Works until 1960, when it moved to the Southern Region to work the Weymouth Quay Branch. When replaced there by diesels in August 1962, No. 1369 was transferred, along with classmates No's 1367/68, to Wadebridge shed to work the Wenford Bridge china clay branch in Cornwall, replacing the ancient Beattie 'Well tanks' until diesels took over at the end of 1964.

A smart looking Stourbridge-allocated '28xx' 2-8-0, No. 3825, awaits its next turn of duty outside the roundhouse on 18th February 1962. It would move to Banbury in October of that year and be withdrawn from Oswestry in September 1964, having only been there for two months.

11 – Birmingham to Wolverhampton – London Midland Region

The main line from Birmingham to Wolverhampton originated with the Grand Junction Railway, which built what was Britain's first long distance railway between Newton Junction, near Warrington, and Birmingham, running via Wolverhampton, Bescot and Perry Barr. It was known as the Grand Junction because it joined the Liverpool & Manchester Railway with the London & Birmingham Railway. The original GJR station at Wolverhampton was renamed Wednesfield Heath in 1852, when the Stour Valley line including Wolverhampton (later High Level) station was opened from New Street to Bushbury. Wednesfield Heath closed in 1873.

Opened in 1837, the GJR's Vauxhall terminus was a temporary affair, as the line was completed to Curzon Street eighteen months later. The later Vauxhall station (now Duddeston) opened in 1869. The Grand Junction became part of the L&NWR when that company was formed in 1846.

The Stour Valley line provided an alternative route from Birmingham to Wolverhampton and was proposed by the Birmingham, Wolverhampton & Stour Valley Railway but it was actually built by the L&NWR and opened in 1852.

What became known as the 'Soho Loop' came into being in 1889, when a short section of line was built by the L&NWR to link the Grand Junction and Stour Valley lines, with triangular junctions at each end. These provided great operational flexibility by creating a circular route from New Street around the north of Birmingham, as can be seen from the map; it was electrified in 1966 and is still in use today. It was originally intended to be a freight line but two passenger stations were added in 1896, Soho Road and Handsworth Wood, although both closed in 1941.

The Grand Junction Railway through Bescot by-passed nearby Walsall, although the town later became the junction of six routes. The L&NWR opened a large marshalling yard at Bescot in 1881 and this is still in use today. The major running sheds were at Monument Lane in the centre of Birmingham, Bushbury at Wolverhampton, Bescot and Ryecroft at Walsall.

Soho Loop

A Derby 'Lightweight' two-car DMU working a Walsall to Birmingham service and travelling south towards Soho Road, on the now electrified ex-L&NWR Soho Loop line. It is passing the site of Handsworth Wood station, which closed in 1941. The white building directly above the unit is the Endwood Public House on Hamstead Road, Handsworth.

Perry Barr

Fowler 2-6-4T No. 42346 on a Walsall to Birmingham local at Perry Barr in 1953. It was allocated to Stafford until late 1958.

Stanier 2-6-4T No. 42538 on a Walsall to Birmingham ordinary passenger train near Perry Barr in the early 1950s. It was allocated to Ryecroft shed from July 1952, until transferred to Stafford in September 1954 and then moved on to Bangor in July 1958. The first vehicle is very interesting, being one of the two former L&NWR Holywell 'motor train' coaches to Diagram M3. These were formerly 42ft 0in x 8ft 0in Sleeping (later Picnic) Saloons, built in 1885 and converted for 'pull push' or 'motor' working. We think that the coach is the former L&NWR No. 2136A in (unrecorded) departmental use. It was re-numbered No. 10582 and then No. 975 by the LM&SR and was withdrawn in February 1935. It appears to be in excellent condition after nearly twenty years in departmental service with either the Civil or more likely the Signal & Telegraph Engineers, perhaps as some sort of test or observation vehicle. That would explain the chap looking out of a door droplight holding a trilby hat in his hand – typical attire of mid-level railway managers. We are sure it is not carrying fare-paying passengers and, despite the headlamps, this might even be an Empty Coaching Stock movement.

Witton

English Electric Type '4' No. D323 heading the 'Pines Express' on 28th June 1962 at Witton, before it was re-routed via Shrewsbury, Wellington and Wolverhampton from September 1962. After this date, English Electric Type '4's only worked the train as far as Wolverhampton before handing over to a Western Region 'Castle' to take it to Oxford, where another engine change was effected.

Birmingham Division (D02) allocated BR Sulzer Type '2' No. D7670 passing through Witton with the 8T69 trip working on 6th October 1967. This was the 11.35 Bescot Up Yard-Curzon Street, dropping off cripples at Vauxhall Carriage & Wagon Works, whilst the 'Presflos' were for the Castle Cement terminal at Curzon Street. No. D7670 was one of the last batch of Derby-built Sulzers. These were part of an order given to Beyer-Peacock but their worsening financial position led to that company asking for a release from construction of the final eighteen locomotives. Built in Rail Blue livery with full yellow ends and fitted with three-part miniature snow ploughs, No. D7670 was only nine months old here but had already been allocated to the London and Nottingham divisions. Withdrawal came as No. 25320 in December 1983 at Derby and it was cut-up at Swindon in June 1985. The headquarters of Imperial Metal Industries Ltd is a notable background feature of Witton station.

Monument Lane Shed

The ex-L&NWR shed was only a short distance outside New Street, on the Stour Valley line to Wolverhampton alongside the Birmingham Main Line Canal, on the site where the National Indoor Arena now stands. The six road shed was built in 1858, with two pitched roofs instead of the standard L&NWR northlight design and was accessed off a headshunt. A new 60 foot turntable was installed in the 1920s and the LM&SR added coaling and ash plants in 1934, and a water softening plant in 1938. Its allocation was mainly tank engines and freight locomotives, with a handful of passenger engines, notably 'Compound' 4-4-0s and later Stanier Class '5's, Bushbury and Camden providing motive power for the expresses between London and the West Midlands. The shed

provided the station pilots for the 'Western' side of New Street station, with Saltley or Bournville sheds covering the 'Midland' side. In the early 1950s, these were ex-L&NWR 0-6-2T 'Coal Tanks', which were followed by Stanier 2-6-2Ts until the diesels took over. All of the shed's steam locomotives were transferred away in February 1962, leaving just diesel shunters on its books, no main line diesels being allocated there. The carriage shed was converted for use as a diesel depot in 1956, the first diesel shed in the area, when Diesel Multiple Units were introduced on the Lichfield service. Monument Lane shed closed in March 1967. It was coded 3E from 1935 and 21E in 1960 until September 1963, when it became 2H.

A fairly empty Monument Lane shed on 27th November 1960, with only a 2-6-4T and a diesel shunter visible.

'Compound' No. 40933 rests at its home shed, with the unique curved top tender built in May 1935 on a standard 3,500 gallon underframe. This ran for many years behind 'Compound' No. 936 but, in January 1954, was transferred to No. 40933, with which it remained until July 1957; it was then paired with No. 40926. No. 40933 was allocated to Monument Lane from 1951 until the end of 1957.

No. 41168, the last 'Compound' in British Railways stock, pictured on 19th March 1961 when in store at Monument Lane, before it went to Derby for scrapping. It was not formally withdrawn until July.

Stanier Class '4MT' 2-6-4T No. 42488 over the pits at Monument Lane on 19th March 1961. It was in its second spell there, moving from Bushbury in August 1958, although it went into store almost immediately and stayed out of service until June 1959. It eventually left for Aston in February 1962.

Although numerically the third Stanier Class '5', No. 44660, pictured on 19th March 1961 at Monument Lane, was one of the last ten built at Crewe in 1949 and was allocated to Saltley throughout its life, being withdrawn in August 1964.

Bescot

The London & North Western Railway's extensive new sorting sidings at Bescot were completed in 1892 and the shed to service them was built at the same time. Bescot was always a freight shed, with forty-nine out of its seventy-strong allocation being 8-coupled locomotives in 1954. The LM&SR equipped the shed with a unique mechanical coaling plant constructed by the Wellman-Owen Corp at nearby Darlaston in 1936, together with a new ash plant to a more common design. The shed was coded 3A, denoting its importance as the 'concentration' depot for the

Western Division of the LM&SR in the Birmingham area. It was re-roofed in 1949-50, re-coded 21B in 1960 and again to 2F in 1963. The shed closed to steam at the end of March 1966 but a new diesel refuelling and maintenance depot was constructed on part of the yard. Strangely, the shell of the steam shed survived into the 21st century complete with trees growing through the roof. The yard was rebuilt in 1965 at a cost of £1.5million, to handle an estimated 4,000 wagons a day and is still in use today.

'Jubilee' No. 45638 *Zanzibar* passing through Bescot with a Birmingham-Glasgow express in 1952.

Stanier '8F' No. 48368, seen here in the early 1960s, has large 10ins cab numbers and also the final type of Fowler 3,500 gallon tender with coal rails and snap head rivets that it received in mid-1961, which was noticeably narrower than the engine's cab. The picture shows lots of good detail, including the windshields on the cab windows, the sandbox fillers, the reversing rod and the AWS conduit.

A clean Class '5', No. 44765 from Crewe North shed which is coupled with a roller bearing fitted, part-welded tender, is seen shunting wagons under the ash disposal plant at Bescot on 18th February 1962. In the background is the distinctive coaling plant.

Ex-L&NWR 'G2' 0-8-0 No. 48964 was a Bescot engine from May 1951 until withdrawn in April 1962. The old Bescot station and footbridge are just visible to the left. Note the wartime white painted lamp on the right, whilst the 'G2' is still fitted with the early pattern three-piece coupling rods, a very late use of these.

Ex-LM&SR '8F' 2-8-0 No. 48713 also arrived at Bescot in 1951, from Newton Heath, and remained there until January 1966, when it was transferred to Nuneaton. It is in final condition with AWS, which had been fitted in October 1960, Overhead Line Warning flashes, external pipework to the steam lance cock on the smokebox and a lowered top lamp bracket. This picture was probably taken in 1964 or 1965, since rebuilding work for electrification is clearly underway with a new footbridge already in place. No. 48713 was built for the L&NER in July 1944 at the Southern Railway's Brighton Works. It carried three different numbers before it became No. 8713 in December 1947, starting with No. 7659 when built, No. 3108 in April 1946 and No. 3508 in February 1947. The picture gives a good view of the position of the coaler and ash towers and in the distance the footbridges of the new station; work on the platforms is underway.

Class 'G2' 0-8-0 No. 49328 was at Bescot for many years and was eventually withdrawn from there in late 1962. This rear view is interesting because it shows an unusual fitting at the front of the Bowen-Cooke tender, a three-piece steel angle which was probably intended to prevent the footplate crew from going near to live overhead wires. The device is also on the Fowler tender of the '4F' in front of the 'G2'.

Super power as 'G2' No. 49173 and '8F' No. 48764 drag a long freight northwards out of Bescot yard in 1963. The 'G2' was one of the last four of the former L&NWR 0-8-0s to be found working out their final days from Bescot in 1964. They were diagrammed for three duties in the summer schedules, which commenced on 13th June.

Walsall

After Walsall was bypassed by the Grand Junction Railway in 1837, it was ten years before this important town was connected to the railway, when the South Staffordshire Railway (SSR) opened a temporary station there. Two years later, a permanent station was built when its line to Dudley was completed. On 1st February 1858, the SSR opened the line to Cannock from Rycroft Junction, Walsall, which was extended to Rugeley on 7th November the following year. The line was formally absorbed into the L&NWR in 1869. In 1872, the Wolverhampton & Walsall Railway opened a line to Wolverhampton, which was initially operated jointly by the Midland Railway and the London & North Western Railway. After numerous disagreements, it was bought by the London & North Western Railway in 1875 but a year later was sold to the Midland Railway, who then connected it to its Sutton Park Line.

The original station was becoming badly congested and was rebuilt by the L&NWR in 1883 and again in the early 1920s, after extensive fire damage in 1916. By the mid-1960s, Walsall was reduced to just one remaining passenger service, to Birmingham, and the station site was redeveloped in 1978 as a shopping centre, with these trains using a basic halt nearby. Then followed a renaissance which saw firstly the reinstatement of the Walsall to Hednesford service, which was subsequently extended to Rugeley and then Stafford, and the short lived re-opening of the Walsall to Wolverhampton service in 1998.

Tender first ex-London & North Western Railway 'G2' No. 49114 pilots an unidentified classmate on the Down Slow through Walsall Station in 1961. The view is looking towards Pleck Junction, with Walsall No 2 box on the left. The pair were probably working the Target 224 Class '7' Freight, the 9.00am Bescot Old Yard-Wichnor Sidings, with the Target 372 engine coupled on as far as Norton Junction. No. 49114 was allocated to Bescot from May 1958 until transferred to Edge Hill in November 1961. The safety bar at the top front of its tender has been inscribed with 'Hot Dogs 3d each'!

A Gloucester Railway Carriage & Wagon Company two-car DMU, Class '100' under TOPS, parked in the centre road at Walsall, with 'Wolverhampton HL' on its destination blind and 21F, the depot code for nearby Ryecroft from June 1960 until September 1963, on its bufferbeam. Nearest the camera is Driving Motor Brake Second No. M50349.

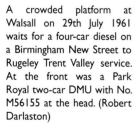

A crowded platform at Walsall on 29th July 1961 waits for a four-car diesel on a Birmingham New Street to Rugeley Trent Valley service. At the front was a Park Royal two-car DMU with No. M56155 at the head. (Robert Darlaston)

Wednesbury Town

Two freight trains pass at Wednesbury Town in late 1963 or early 1964, the one on the right, going towards Dudley, headed by Stanier '8F' 2-8-0 No. 48478. It was shedded at Stourbridge Junction as indicated by the code 2C, which came into effect in September 1963, painted on its smokebox door.

Wednesbury Town, the ex-L&NWR station known as plain 'Wednesbury' up to 1950, with a Birmingham Railway Carriage & Wagon Company DMU, later Class '104', arriving from Walsall and going to Dudley on 4th July 1964, the last day of the service. Wednesbury No. 2 signal box, visible to the right of the train, was a former South Staffordshire Railway box. (Robert Darlaston)

Dudley Port

Despite its name, Dudley Port is not actually in the town of Dudley. The name emerged during the 19th century as a result of the large number of warehouses and wharfs which developed around the Birmingham Canal, to serve the growing industries in nearby Dudley. The area was originally known as Dudley's Port but soon became shortened to Dudley Port.

Dudley Port (Low Level) station was opened in 1850 by the South Staffordshire Railway, later absorbed by the L&NWR. The Birmingham & Shrewsbury Railway, also absorbed into the L&NWR, opened its Stour Valley route in 1852, which crossed this line, and opened its own station which naturally took the name Dudley Port (High Level). The South Staffordshire line from Dudley to Walsall was closed in 1964, along with the Low Level station and High Level became simply Dudley Port.

Ex-L&NWR 'G2' 0-8-0 No. 49099 approaches Dudley Port High Level with an Up goods on 18th June 1960. The branch to Dudley diverges to the left. (Robert Darlaston)

Class 'AL6' electric No. E3182 south of Dudley Port on 29th May 1967, with the 1A51 13.25 Liverpool-Euston, 14.49 off Wolverhampton, alongside the Birmingham Canal Main Line. It became No. 86245 in April 1974 and carried the name *Dudley Castle* between 1984 and 1998. A British Railways Mark 1 Restaurant car in the middle spoils the appearance of an otherwise uniform rake of the new Mark II coaches; no Mark II catering vehicles were ever built.

Class '5101' 2-6-2T No. 4146 in Dudley Port Low Level station on Saturday 25th July 1959, with the 5.35pm Birmingham Snow Hill to Dudley. The Stour Valley line is clearly visible in the background and High Level station is just in view at the extreme left. (Michael Mensing)

This picture was taken from the overbridge, looking in the opposite direction to the photograph of No. 4146 and shows a Derby Lightweight twin set, later Class '108', on a Walsall to Dudley service at Dudley Port Low Level on 18th June 1960. Ryecroft had six of these two-car sets briefly, delivered between February and May 1960 but they left between December 1960 and July 1961. (Robert Darlaston)

Dudley

Dudley station opened in 1860 and was at the intersection of lines built by the Oxford, Worcester & Wolverhampton Railway and the South Staffordshire Railway – later incorporated into the GWR and L&NWR (itself later absorbed into the LM&SR), respectively.

A Birmingham Railway Carriage & Wagon Company DMU, later Class '104', for Walsall waits for the passengers to board at the former L&NWR platform at Dudley on 4th July 1964. The ex-Great Western platforms to the right are included in Chapter 10. (Robert Darlaston)

Wolverhampton High Level

A Gloucester Railway Carriage & Wagon Company two-car DMU, Class '100' under TOPS, arriving at Wolverhampton High Level with the 4.44pm from Lichfield via Walsall on Saturday 13th September 1958. Mill Street goods station and warehouse is in the right background. (Michael Mensing)

No. 46169 *The Boy Scout* in 1959 or 1960 at Wolverhampton High Level. It was the last 'Royal Scot' built and moved to Crewe North from Longsight in July 1959, at the same date as AWS was fitted. Train reporting number W156 in 1959 was the 9.55am FSX/10.10am FSO Edinburgh Princes Street-Birmingham New Street, which was due to call at Wolverhampton High Level from 4.11 to 4.15pm.

The south end of Wolverhampton High Level in 1964, with a Park Royal DMU on a Lichfield service. The station is in a poor state as work has started to prepare for its rebuilding with the platform canopies already taken out.

Bushbury

The L&NWR first built a shed at Bushbury, on the northern edge of Wolverhampton, in 1859 and it was rebuilt in 1883, doubling its capacity. Although it provided engines for the London expresses, Bushbury was always in the shadow of the nearby Great Western shed at Stafford Road. It was coded 3B until June 1960, when it became 21C, changed again to 2K in September 1963 and was closed in April 1965.

'Royal Scot' No. 46142 *The York and Lancaster Regiment* passing Bushbury Cold Store in 1959, as it leaves Bushbury on the Up Grand Junction line towards Wednesfield Heath and Bescot. This locomotive had started life as Lion in November 1927, was renamed in May 1936, rebuilt with a taper boiler in 1951 and was fitted with AWS in September 1959, after this picture was taken. No. 46142 was allocated to Edge Hill from October 1955 until September 1959, when it moved to Kentish Town.

A pristine shed favourite, 'Jubilee' No. 45738 *Samson*, at Bushbury in 1958, its home shed since 1951. Bushbury had nine 'Jubilees' used almost exclusively on the London expresses. Camden on the other hand tended to use its rebuilt '7Ps', either 'Royal Scots' or 'Patriots', for their West Midlands diagrams. No. 45738 moved to Carlisle Upperby in November 1959, after the through services between Wolverhampton and London were transferred to the Western Region when electrification work began on the London Midland route.

12 – South West of Birmingham

The lines on the south west side of the city were under the control of the Midland Railway, except for the short L&NWR branch to Harborne. First came the Birmingham & Gloucester Railway, opened in 1841, with its main line over the Lickey Incline reaching Birmingham via Kings Heath, Moseley and Camp Hill into Curzon Street station. A branch line from Barnt Green to Redditch was added in 1859 and this was later extended to Evesham. In 1876, the Birmingham West Suburban Railway was opened from New Street to Kings Norton through Selly Oak, where it joined the line from Camp Hill.

In 1885, the Stirchley Street & Bournville to Kings Norton Deviation was completed, which allowed Midland Railway trains from Derby to Bristol to run directly through Birmingham, instead of having to change engines and reverse direction. In the south, after passing through the renamed Bournville and Stirchley station, the line swung westwards away from the canal after passing under Mary Vale Road Bridge, to join the Birmingham & Gloucester line to the north east of Kings Norton station, providing a more direct and flatter route between Kings Norton and the Birmingham West Suburban Railway. In the north, it connected New Street via tunnels under both Gloucester Row and Bath Row, and then via Five Ways to the Birmingham West Suburban Railway.

In 1892, a curve was built at Lifford joining the Camp Hill and West Suburban lines, which allowed the Midland Railway to run a circular passenger service from New Street and back via Bournville,

Lifford and Camp Hill. The local service on the Camp Hill line, including the Lifford Loop trains, was withdrawn in 1941 to relieve congestion on the main line and, although intended to be a temporary wartime measure, the closure was made permanent in 1946. Although some excursions or similar passenger trains avoiding New Street ran via the Camp Hill line, the line was and remains primarily a freight route to this day.

Harborne

The short 2 miles and 35 chain Harborne Branch, running from a junction near Monument Lane, was opened in 1874 by the Harborne Railway Company, which contracted to the L&NWR to operate the line on its behalf. Initially it was very successful but was subsequently closed to passengers in 1934 due to competition from trams and buses. Freight traffic lingered on up to 1964, partly because it gave access to Mitchells & Butlers Brewery sidings.

This view from on board the railtour behind No. 58271 was taken as it was waiting to rejoin the main line near Monument Lane on the return journey from Harborne; No. 58283 was at the rear of the train. No. 58271 had been at Crewe South since late 1957 but was transferred to Monument Lane at the beginning of May 1959, presumably to work the tour; it was withdrawn in June 1961. (Robert Darlaston)

Midland Railway '2F' 0-6-0 No. 58283 after travelling down the short freight only branch to Harborne with the Stephenson Locomotive Society's 'Golden Jubilee' railtour from Birmingham New Street on 30th May 1959. Another '2F', No. 58271, was at the rear of the six ex-LM&SR corridor coaches. No. 58283 was at Ryecroft (Walsall) from late 1950 until June 1958, when it moved to Bescot; it was withdrawn in March 1961. The two '2Fs' took the train from New Street to Harborne and then on to Old Hill and Halesowen, via Aston, Perry Barr and Soho. They returned to New Street via Longbridge and Kings Norton. The tour continued using a Metropolitan-Cammell DMU and visiting many by-ways of the Black Country, Bournville and even Birmingham Central goods depot. (Robert Darlaston)

Selly Oak

Unrebuilt 'Patriot' No. 45506 *The Royal Pioneer Corps* with a Birmingham bound express on 24th March 1961, next to the Worcester & Birmingham Canal between Selly Oak and Bournville. No. 45506 was at Bristol Barrow Road from November 1958 until withdrawn in March 1962.

Bournville

Above left: Bournville was a shed long associated with ancient motive power. It provided locomotives for the GWR/LM&SR joint line from Longbridge to Halesowen with its severe weight restriction, so small light engines were the order of the day. Surplus locomotives had been stored at the shed since the 1930s, when ex-MR 'Flatiron' 0-6-4Ts, once regulars on the Birmingham suburban trains, were laid up here. Saltley '3F' No. 43214, with classmate No. 43507 behind, continue the tradition, stored stripped of vacuum pipe hoses but fully coaled, probably in 1959 or 1960 before No. 43214 was withdrawn in June 1961. The shed itself was closed in February 1960.

Above right: 'Compound' No. 41048 from Wellingborough in the roundhouse at Bournville on 3rd August 1957. It was very near to the end of its working life, being taken out of service in October of that year.

BR Standard '5MT' No. 73054 at Bournville on 8th September 1957. Its train comprises mostly ex-L&NER stock, with an odd BR Mark 1 and ex-GWR coach mixed in. No. 73054 went to Bristol Barrow Road in May 1957 and remained there until transferred to its final shed at Bath Green Park.

King's Norton

Opened in 1849, Kings Norton is one of the oldest stations on today's 'Cross City' line, on what was originally the Birmingham & Gloucester Railway's line from the south to Curzon Street via the Camp Hill route. With the coming of the Birmingham West Suburban Railway's Kings Norton Extension in 1892, the station was expanded to three platforms and a level crossing that carried Station Road across the tracks was replaced by a footbridge. A large coal and goods yard was also built, with sidings for the adjacent Triplex Works.

Fowler 2-6-4T No. 42326 at Kings Norton on a Redditch to Birmingham New Street local in the mid-1950s. No. 42326 was at Saltley throughout the early 1950s but was transferred to Derby in October 1957.

Another Saltley engine, 'Crab' 2-6-0 No. 42827, arriving at Kings Norton with a southbound train. It stayed longer than No. 42326, moving away to Birkenhead Mollington Street in June 1964.

BR Sulzer Type '2' No. D7592 is approaching Kings Norton station and crossing to the Up Camp Hill line in the mid-1960s. Its headcode of 9T28 shows that it is on the T28 trip, working around the Kings Norton area, from and to Washwood Heath.

Northfield

An Oxley '2884' Class 2-8-0, No. 3813, on the Up goods line at Northfield. The signal box, which is on the south or Barnt Green side of the station, is largely obscured by the engine, while the goods sidings are to the left. The train will have come from either Worcester or Gloucester and would be heading for Washwood Heath Up sidings, Lawley Street or Water Orton. The picture was almost certainly taken after the lines south of Barnt Green were 'operationally' transferred to the Western Region on 1st February 1958. Until then, WR territory extended to Church Road Junction but the line was operationally under London Midland Region control.

A Metro-Cammell Class '101' two-car DMU near Northfield on 12th August 1961, on a Birmingham New Street to Redditch train. Even after the service was dieselised in 1960, it still operated independently of the New Street to Lichfield service and it would be nearly two decades later before the West Midlands Passenger Transport Executive finally brought them together in the 'Cross-City' line. After extensive modernisation work and construction of three new stations, services began in May 1978 between Four Oaks and Longbridge. They were subsequently extended to Lichfield in the north and Redditch in the south, with the whole route electrified by 1993, producing the excellent and frequent service which runs today.

Longbridge and the Halesowen Branch

Midland Railway '2F' 0-6-0 No. 58138 on the Halesowen branch in 1949. No. 58138 was at Bournville shed throughout the 1950s, finally moving away to Bushbury in February 1960. The branch was jointly worked by the Great Western Railway and the Midland Railway, and opened in 1883, with stations at Longbridge, Rubery and Hunnington operated by the joint companies, before reaching the Great Western station at Halesowen. Midland freight trips only ran between Longbridge and Halesowen. This is probably Target 72 returning to Longbridge from Halesowen.

The branch from Longbridge wound its way through relatively unspoilt countryside on Birmingham's western fringes to Halesowen and Old Hill, where it joined the Great Western's Stourbridge line. Public passenger services had been withdrawn in 1927 but two daily trains survived until August 1958 to take workers to and from the Austin Motor Company's Longbridge works. In this picture, taken from Longbridge Signal Box, '74xx' 0-6-0PT No. 7448 from Stourbridge Junction, is setting off for Old Hill with the penultimate train on 29th August 1958, the 5.09pm from Longbridge. (Robert Darlaston)

Another Stourbridge Junction '74xx', No. 7430, approaching Longbridge bunker first with empty stock for the final 5.40pm workmen's train to Old Hill on 29th August 1958, the last day of the service, although a similar working from Longbridge to Birmingham New Street lasted until the end of 1959. The sidings on the right served the Austin Motor Company factory. (Robert Darlaston)

The Austin Motor Company factory established at Longbridge in 1905 was situated adjacent and south of the joint line to Halesowen. At the start of the First World War, the site was converted to military work, including munitions, and rail sidings were laid in 1915. Expansion was rapid and soon extended to three factories on both sides of the line. These were appropriately named the North, South and West Works, each having a locomotive shed. Austin exercised its rights to purchase the properties at the end of the war and turned over the buildings initially to large-scale tractor production. The West Works shed was closed but as operations either side of the railway branch were independent, the other two sheds continued in use. The heaviest work was to the north, where the large Bagnall saddle tanks were the last steam engines operated. Diesels started arriving from 1969, including new locomotives, ones transferred from other plants and an ex-BR Class '08' shunter, and the Bagnalls were not used after 1972. Locomotives now worked over BR metals, marshalling car trains in the sidings of the truncated Halesowen Branch, as well as continuing the internal traffic including moving coal from the stockpile to the boiler house.

Abernant was built by Manning Wardle in Leeds in 1921, Works No. 2015, for Cardiff Corporation, who used it on the Llwynon Reservoir construction project. It was sold via T. W. Ward Ltd to the Austin Motor Company in December 1927 and worked at Longbridge until 1963, when it became surplus and was purchased by J. Cashmore's, Great Bridge. However, it was not scrapped and was presented to a children's playground at Duddeston in inner-city Birmingham early in 1964. It was removed to Tyseley in 1989 and has since moved around various preservation sites.

Vulcan, Works No. 2994, was one of three engines built by Bagnalls of Stafford in 1950 for the Steel Corporation of Wales, for their Abbey, Margam and Port Talbot works. They were probably the most advanced industrial engines ever built in the United Kingdom, and had outside cylinders with Walschaerts valve gear, rocking grates, self-cleaning smokeboxes, twin brake blocks and roller bearings throughout. When diesels took over in 1957, two of them were sold to Austin at Longbridge and named *Victor* and *Vulcan*. This view was probably taken soon after arrival, with one of the two Hunslet Engine Company locomotives, either *Austin 2* or *Austin 3* behind. They were painted in dark green with yellow lining and given the Austin heraldic device, which caused the works plates to be moved to the top of the saddle tank support. Both were preserved and originally went to the West Somerset Railway but were ousted when that railway brought in main line locomotives. *Vulcan* was sold to the Metropolitan Borough of Tyneside for use at its Stephenson Museum and renamed *Thomas Burt MP 1837-1922*, and is still there today.

Barnt Green

Saltley Class '5' No. 44966, running under Class 'C' (parcels, fish, livestock, milk, fruit or perishables) headlamps, at Barnt Green, looking towards Birmingham from the Up main line platform. The picture was taken some time between September 1963, when Saltley became 2E as painted on the engine's smokebox door, and April 1964, when it was transferred to Aston.

Class 8F' 2-8-0 No. 48350 approaches Barnt Green with a Class 'J' Down mineral train on 18th March 1961. The '8F' was built at Horwich Works in April 1944 and spent most of its life at Toton, before moving to Kettering in June 1964. The junction for the branch to Redditch and Evesham is in the foreground. (Robert Darlaston)

Redditch

Redditch was on the Midland Railway branch from Barnt Green; it was originally opened as a terminus in 1859 but became a through station when the line was extended to Evesham in 1868. British Railways closed the line south of Alcester in September 1962, after suspending the passenger service between Redditch and Evesham due to the poor condition of the track, although freight services continued until 1964. Services to Redditch from Birmingham followed a similar pattern of rise and fall as those on the Lichfield line, with which it later joined as part of the Birmingham 'Cross-City' line. The number of trains fell from

a daily peak of seventeen in 1938. The service did not increase until diesel multiple units took over the Redditch trains in April 1960; the trains to Evesham remained steam hauled until they ceased in 1962. There were eighteen trains, approximately hourly but, perversely, just when Redditch had been designated as a New Town, British Railways published a notice of closure in August 1964. This was rejected but the service was reduced in 1966 to only three trains each way per day and it struggled on until finally it was electrified in 1992, following the extension of the 'Cross-City' line southwards from Longbridge.

Redditch station looking north on 7th May 1966, with a Metropolitan-Cammell two-car DMU, Class '101' under TOPS, to Birmingham New Street. The service had been improved with regular interval hourly trains when diesel multiple units replaced steam in April 1960 but it would be 1993 before it was transformed with the completion of the 'Cross-City' electrification. (Robert Darlaston)

The Lickey Incline

The two miles of 1 in 37¾ gradient of the Lickey Incline on the Bristol to Birmingham line was the result of its original builder, the Birmingham & Gloucester Railway, deciding to take the most 'direct' route between Cheltenham and Birmingham. From its opening in 1840 through until the end of steam on British Railways, special working arrangements were needed to operate traffic over this busy main line. Banking engines were stationed at Bromsgrove to assist anything but the lightest northbound train up the hill to Blackwell. The best known of these was the unique 0-10-0 No. 58100, christened 'Big Bertha' after the huge First World War German howitzer, which was built by the Midland Railway in 1914 specifically for use on the Lickey. The other banking engines from the late 1920s until the mid-1950s were standard LM&SR 'Jinty' 0-6-0Ts. When No. 58100 had to be withdrawn in 1956 with a worn crank axle, it was replaced by a BR '9F' 2-10-0, No. 92079. The 'Jinties', apart from two which lingered on until 1964, were ousted by Western Region '94xx' "Pannier" tanks in late 1956. These lasted until September 1964, when Bromsgrove shed closed and English Electric Type '3' diesels took over the banking.

No. 47425 and two other 'Jinty' bankers returning down the incline to Bromsgrove in 1953. No. 47425 left Bromsgrove in December 1956, when the Western Region '94xx' "Pannier"'s arrived.

A single 'Jinty' on its way down in March 1961, on its own unusually, since returning bankers were normally worked back together, albeit uncoupled. No. 47276 was transferred in late 1950 from Saltley and was one of the last two of the class to work the incline, leaving in April 1964 for Bath Green Park, along with No. 47308.

Class '3F' 0-6-0 No. 43186 in the early 1950s in front of No. 58100 'Big Bertha' on Bromsgrove shed; the latter's name was unofficial. No. 43186 had been transferred here from Hellifield in October 1950 and was one of the '3F's with slightly smaller wheels, 4ft 11ins compared to the 5ft 2ins of the majority of the class. Note the tarpaulin rolled back on the cab roof.

A fine study of No. 58100 in action in the early 1950s. The coaches, from right to left, are a real mixture of styles: a Stanier Brake followed by a Gresley side corridor Third, then two examples of early LM&SR built stock. Next is a very interesting ex-Great Eastern Railway BG (a Bogie Gangwayed Parcels coach, which became L&NER diagram 548E). This had been converted from First World War Ward Cars from No. 75 Ambulance Train and appears to be still in wartime brown from World War Two. At the rear there is a Southern Railway designed PMV (Parcel & Miscellaneous Van).

The ex-LN&ER Garratt No. 69999, which had been used to bank trains up the Worsborough Incline on the Barnsley avoiding line since its introduction in 1925, was sent to Bromsgrove in March 1949. Its future was in doubt because of the condition of its boiler and the forthcoming electrification of the Worsborough route as part of the Woodhead electrification, so the Lickey represented the only alternative employment for such a machine. For the first few days there it was used chimney first but, after complaints from the crews who said they could not judge the distance when buffering up to a train, it was turned around. The picture appears to have been taken before this happened. No. 69999 went back to the Eastern Region in November 1950, where it was stored at Mexborough for three months before resuming its old duties. In 1952, it went into Gorton Works, staying for three years while it was converted for oil burning. No. 69999 finally emerged in June 1955 and returned to the Lickey very briefly and unsuccessfully, before it was returned to Gorton in October and was withdrawn by the end of the year.

'Big Bertha' in 1955 doing what she was designed to do. The locomotive had been painted in the new BR mixed traffic lined black livery in May 1950. Lining was not applied to the Bromsgrove 'Jinty' 0-6-0Ts, which retained their plain black livery. No. 58100 would be withdrawn the following year after almost forty years continuous service on this single duty. Its tender was rebuilt from a MR 2,350 gallon tender and held 2,050 gallons of water and 4 tons of coal; the sides had been cut-down in 1926 to improve visibility when running tender first and to make coaling easier. The tender cab was fitted to provide protection for the footplatemen when returning light engine to Bromsgrove.

No. 58100 had four cylinders to produce the required power and was by far the largest engine built by the Midland Railway, with a tractive effort of 43,000lbs. The outside cylinders were inclined at an angle of 1 in 7 to ensure that all the connecting rods drove on the centre axle. The vertical stanchions at the corners of the front footplate were provided to assist drivers to judge the distance when buffering up to passenger trains, with an electric headlight for use in the dark. Some drivers allegedly switched the light off, since it alerted the crew on the train they were to assist that it was 'Big Bertha' buffering up and they thus might not work their engine as hard as if it was being banked by the tank engines. The new cylinders fitted in 1954 to No. 58100, after the originals were damaged when water got into the left-hand inside cylinder, are evident in this photograph. The spare set had been cast when the engine was built but had lain forgotten in a dusty corner of Derby Works for forty years. So 'Big Bertha' was reprieved but this was short-lived and it was withdrawn in May 1956, when the crank axle journals were found to be worn beyond scrapping limits and this time even Derby had no spares tucked away.

All passenger trains of more than three coaches had to be banked up the incline. Ivatt '4MT' No. 43047 is assisted with its six coach local by a single 'Jinty'. The 2-6-0 was at Saltley from June 1953 until September 1962 and received its single chimney in December 1954. In the left a little way down from the 'Jinty', another banker, possibly the '9F', can just be discerned descending light engine down the incline.

Bristol Barrow Road 'Jubilee' No. 45660 *Rooke* on an express in the mid-1950s, which is being banked by two 'Jinties'. The number of banking engines used was determined by the weight of the train, with the rules set out in the Working Time Table.

An interesting quintet of the '9F' No. 92079 and three 'Jinty' bankers sandwiching a '3F' 0-6-0, makes its way down the incline on a summer's day watched by dad and one son; the other is busying looking the other way. Note the trap point on the left hand track to catch runaways separated from trains travelling up the incline.

Bromsgrove South engine siding had a manual coaling stage and the locomotives were prepared in strict order, to ensure all the drivers and fireman did the same amount of work. The '9F' and two out of the three 'Panniers' nearest the camera have built up plenty of steam ready for their next bout of banking. A fourth one waits in the distance, about to cross over to start its next stint of work. No. 92079 had been built with a BR 1C tender with high curved top sidesheets but this was exchanged in May 1956 when it was transferred to Bromsgrove, for the BR 1G type shown, which gave better visibility when running tender first back down the incline.

BR-built '94xx' No. 8405 has buffered up and is starting off on its two mile climb up to Blackwell. It arrived here at Bromsgrove in December 1956 from Duffryn Yard and remained until withdrawn in September 1964.

No. 8402 and another '94xx' are half-way up the incline assisting a heavy passenger train. No. 8402 came to Bromsgrove from Cardiff Canton in August 1956 and left for Gloucester Horton Road in September 1964, only to be withdrawn a few weeks later. Unlike most of its classmates, it was probably worn out after its exertions on the Lickey.

Four bankers, two ex-LMS 'Jinties' and two ex-GWR '94xx' 0-6-0PTs, ease their way back down from Blackwell in 1958. At the rear is No. 8404, which arrived at Bromsgrove in December 1956 and was withdrawn from there in November 1961. The 'Jinties' were two of the last three survivors of the class at the shed, No's 47276, 47308 and 47313. Note the Target boards, 6 on No. 8404, and 8 on the nearest 'Jinty'.

No. 8405 and an unidentified classmate near the top of the incline in 1963.

Saltley-based '4F' No. 43940 slogs its way up the incline watched by a number of passengers. The leading coaches are a pair of L&NER articulated non corridor suburbans. Train M258 would be a Saturdays Only train, a Paignton-York or similar, or more likely a relief to one such, and is pre-1962 when four digit headcodes were introduced. No. 43940 was paired from March 1951 with a snap-head riveted Fowler 3,500 gallon tender, in place of the Johnson 3,250 gallon tender it was built with.

No. 92079 in 1963 nearly at the summit of the bank. Over the years, several other '9Fs' were used to cover the Lickey banking duties on the occasions when No. 92079 went into works.

The lady with her shopping waits for the '9F' to reverse over the foot crossing at Blackwell to return down to Bromsgrove. No. 92079 was carrying the F10 Target board which was a WR identity, so this would be after the shed passed to Western Region control on 1st February 1958 but it is not fitted with the headlight from 'Big Bertha'.

A view 'over the top', looking down the incline from Blackwell in the 1950s, as a lone spotter waits for a train coming up from Bromsgrove. This is a good view of the signalling at the top of the incline, with the 'GOODS TRAINS TO STOP TO PIN DOWN BRAKES' board in front of the brakesmen's hut on the left. Bob Essery recalls that all trains which required the brakes to be pinned down needed to be on the falling gradient, otherwise it would not be possible to start the train moving again. All the brake levers had to be dropped but only the prescribed number pinned down. Note the line of Midland Railway lamp posts fitted with replacement 'Mexican hat' gas lamps to provide light for the brakesmen during the hours of darkness.

'Royal Scot' No. 46106 *Gordon Highlander* seems to have left all the work to the bankers as it clears the summit at Blackwell in March 1961. It was the only one of the class with BR type smoke deflectors, fitted in 1954, which were much more effective than the smaller type which all the other rebuilt 'Scots' received. It had been equipped with AWS in October 1959 and was half way through a six-month spell at Trafford Park shed.

Fowler 2-6-4T No. 42422 commences its descent of the bank with a local or more correctly, Ordinary Passenger Train, from Birmingham in May 1961. It was allocated to Saltley from August 1960 until withdrawn in December 1962. Note the 'calling-on' arm below the Down Starter – it was used to allow returning bankers to return to Bromsgrove more quickly than they otherwise could under normal block working. By using permissive working, where more than one train was allowed in a block section, they could follow a freight train down the incline.

Class '5' No. 44852 after descending the incline in 1963, looking towards Bromsgrove station with Bromsgrove South signal box to the right of the train. No. 44852 was at Saltley from July 1951 but then moved to Leeds Holbeck in November 1953 and remained there until it was withdrawn. Note the line from the right into the siding from the Down Fast, which enabled returning bankers to cross over and move clear of the Up Goods (the line next to the 'Panniers').

The train engine and the rear "Pannier", No. 9401, are emitting plenty of smoke and steam but the front banker appears to be taking it easy. The ideal was light grey – too much smoke means not enough air. The exhaust will tell a driver how good or bad the combustion is. No. 9401 was at Bromsgrove from November 1962 until withdrawn the following July.

Front and rear views of Western Region 'Hall' No. 6936 *Breccles Hall* being banked by No. 92079. The first picture is an unusual shot of a GWR locomotive, other than the '94xx' bankers, on the incline. It has an 88A shedplate which indicates that the picture was taken in 1961 or 1962, because this was Cardiff Canton's shedcode only from January 1961 until September 1963, and No. 6936 had moved on to Cardiff East Dock by September 1962. It was probably on the 6.10am Class 'D' freight from Cardiff to Lawley Street which used either a Canton 'Hall' or 'Grange'. The train was worked by Saltley men from Worcester and the engine, after servicing at Saltley, returned on the Washwood Heath Sidings to Stoke Gifford Class 'E' goods.

Saltley-based '8F' No. 48351 creeps down the bank in 1963, ready to stop for the brakes to be released. The engine brakes would be fully on, the wagon brakes pinned down and the tender handbrake screwed down. All freight trains descending the incline had to stop at Blackwell so that the prescribed numbers of wagons could have their brakes pinned down. Partly fitted trains had to take at least seven minutes and unfitted trains at least twelve minutes for the descent. Note the five pigeon baskets on the left of the picture – like many stations at this date this would be a regular traffic at Bromsgrove.

Stanier Class '5' No. 44963 on the Down Fast line in 1963. The Down platform at Bromsgrove was on the Down Slow, whereas the Up platform was on the Up Main, because there was only one line through the station in that direction. No. 44963 was allocated to Saltley from November 1954 until April 1964, when it moved to Crewe South. The Regulations covering the working of the incline stated that 'Passenger trains must not descend the incline in less than five minutes, or at a greater speed than twenty-seven miles per hour.'

What are the cameramen at Bromsgrove on 7th April 1963 waiting for? – surely not a common or garden 'Peak', or perhaps they have just visited the shed? A later-built member of what will become Class '45' has just descended the bank with a train from the north east to the south west. The first box of its headcode panel is broken and has a number '4' pasted on; the reporting number should presumably be 1V39, the 10.36am Bradford-Paignton. Note the LM&SR 'Hawkeye' station nameboard painted in Western Region brown and cream colours, and the signal box set low on the platform to allow the signalmen to view the line up the incline under the bridge. From 12th March 1962, the banking of normally loaded passenger trains hauled by diesel locomotives was abolished, following trials where loads of up to twelve coaches were worked without assistance.